Transform Your Boundaries

Sarri Gilman MFT

Transform Your Boundaries / by Sarri Gilman.
ISBN-13: 978-0-9897787-2-5

First Printing, 2014

Island Bound Publishing
SarriGilman.com

Acknowledgements

To Diana and Kelly Lindsay who sang my praises, cheered, and carried my therapy chair to the stage.

Thank you to Deborah Nedelman, Ph.D. for providing guidance on writing as I shaped this book.

Thank you to The Daily Herald for supporting me as a columnist. You gave me the courage and confidence to write.

To my husband Ken for your love and endless support, you are my yes. To Somer and Aliza, Saralyn, Ben and Candice, Barbara and Bob, you are in my heart, your enthusiasm and love is always present.

Thank you to my friends Tammy Green, Karla Siedschlag, Kathy Burgoyne, Ph.D. and Valerie Landsburg for your early support of this project.

When I think about all the people who have been a significant part of my life and the work I do, I have many to thank. I am hoping I have thanked you again and again. There are some people who keep showing up, through all the threads, all the projects, all the years, and they are always by my side. You are my band, I can't imagine doing any of it without you.

This book is dedicated to the people I have had the privilege to work with over the years.

Transforming Your Boundaries

By Sarri Gilman, LMFT

I have created 'people' in this book to illustrate patterns and experiences that are common to many of us. These are not the personal life stories of specific people, though you may find bits and parts of characters similar to your own life experience. This book is filled with the tools I have used to help many people.

Chapter 1

This book grew from a workshop I created to explain how to form boundaries, what works and doesn't work, and the essential lessons for building boundaries. People who attended wanted to record the workshop and record their private sessions with me. I realized they needed a way to revisit the information.

I wrote this book to provide all of the foundational tools you will need. However, because of the dynamic nature of boundaries, it is not possible to learn everything all at once by reading this book or any other book about boundaries. This book is meant to be a place to visit as often as you need. It will help you develop your boundary skills to adapt to your situations and your relationships as you live.

I have an advantage in understanding boundaries because I've been a therapist since 1986. I have watched many people wrestle with issues related to boundaries. During the past twenty years, I have also led three different non-profit organizations. For seven of those years, I facilitated leadership development for professionals in business, government, and non-profits. Over time, I created a map in my head to help people navigate their boundary issues. I learned from the people I worked with, that five years, ten years and even twenty years later, the work we did on boundaries has stayed with them. The lessons stood the test of time. People reported back to me that the map I was using was very useful. I created the Transform Your Boundaries Workshop as a way to teach my map whole, all at once, and allow people to see the big picture. This book is another way to learn the same essential tools from the map that I have used again and again to reliably teach boundary building skills.

I am not just a passive observer of boundary work. I am engaged in it in my own life, my own struggles with boundaries, and have concluded that we are all "in process" in an ongoing way with our boundaries. As long as you are living, you are using whatever skills you have and if you do not have a complete toolset, you may find yourself in an exhausting struggle regarding your boundaries.

Having "good" boundaries is not a permanent state. It's an achievement at a particular point in time when our skills are finally good enough to address the issues and relationships in life in a way that allows us to feel in balance. When someone says, "I have good boundaries", it means she is not feeling out of balance, distraught over someone else, exhausted inside, or in some other way out of sorts. But at any time, a new challenge can arise and that very same person can lose her balance and feel torn inside about her boundaries. When you find yourself unsure about your role, uncertain about what you should do, how to help, or see yourself being drained by a situation, return to your boundary work. Return to this book. There will be something here to help you.

One of the things I've noticed is that we learn how to build boundaries in a particular order. The order is really important. You will find the order or structure presented in this book will guide you through the process. If you attempt to do boundary building without understanding what comes first and what comes next, you will find it much harder and may even think it is impossible.

I've also noticed that certain skills build upon each other. Like learning to play an instrument, or preparing to run a marathon, you don't start out playing at Carnegie Hall, and you don't run 26 miles on your first day. There are beginning steps to everything we master. The same is true for boundaries. There are steps that we must master before we can tackle the biggest boundary challenges.

I find that we all become distressed by the biggest of boundary challenges. I call these **extreme challenges**. People often come to therapy needing help with extreme challenges, such as living with someone who abuses them, a family member with severe mental health issues, addiction in their family, trauma, or other difficult things. Without the right tools, we are stuck with responses that don't fit what we are dealing with. In moments like this, you may think the crazy difficult person you are dealing with is the problem. That is part of the problem, but not really the whole thing. You are having a hard time because you don't have a working set of boundaries for a tough situation.

Imagine going into a dark room with absolutely no knowledge that the light switch is used to turn the light on. You walk into the dark room and you wonder if you jump on the floor, or if you push on the walls, or if you even try to drill holes in the ceiling, will it turn on the light? Then, someone comes in and explains that there is a button on the wall. Every time you want the light on, you push the button and the light will go on. Now you know exactly what to do.

The boundary tools in this book are like the light switch. You just need to know how they work and then you can decide how and when to use them.

To help people with the big boundary challenges, I always need to figure out what foundational boundary skills they have and what lessons they are missing. I've never met anyone who had mastery over extreme boundary challenges at all times. It takes tremendous focus and dedication to improve your boundaries. You have to **choose** this work.

I know you are one of the people who has recognized that this is important to you, maybe even life changing, because you picked up this book. You may have never been taught how to build boundaries. I meet many people who are suffering from the impact of not knowing how to set boundaries. It is not unusual or wrong that you don't really know how to do this. Most people don't know how to do this. It is the basis of many physical health problems, divorces, and even wars.

Let's each make a promise. I promise to give you the toolset you need to improve your boundaries. I want one promise from you. Promise me that you will not skip all the chapters and begin with Extreme Challenges. I know that certain situations and certain people are stressful, and we will work our way toward preparing you to be able to manage them better. The skills you need for extreme challenges are built in sequence. The order is important and there is no shortcut to get there faster. You must have all the foundational skills in place to tackle extreme challenges.

Applying It- Start Here:

Keep a journal of thoughts and notes to yourself as you go through this book.

Begin your journal by writing down why you picked up this book. Be specific. What do you want to learn? Describe the situation where you most need to improve your boundaries.

Whenever I need to work on a boundary, I need to be clear in defining the situation where I need to do my work. Otherwise, it can escape from my attention and I will avoid it or ignore it. Writing it down is important because you can remind yourself to do your boundary work exactly where you know it is needed. In the future, every time you revisit this book, answer this question. This is always your starting point: define the issue.

Journal notes:

Journal notes:

Journal notes:

Chapter 2

Figuring out what your boundaries are and where you need them comes from inside of you. You are born with this awareness. If you watch two-year-olds, you will see they know exactly what No means. It seems we are all born with the awareness of what is really a No for us and what is a Yes.

But from the time we are very young, we are told what our boundaries should be. We are taught rules about what is OK and what is not OK from our family, culture, school, community, perhaps a religion, etc. Our No from inside is tamed and told to be quiet.

Think of your inner self like a radio. We are tuned in to all these voices telling us where our boundaries should be. These voices tell us what is expected of us.

When we go to school, more voices are added about boundaries, and as we get older and leave home, employers tell us where the boundaries are in the workplace.

We are all listening to the radio of other voices – family, school, culture, employer – and it becomes hard to hear our own inner voice. We struggle to hear our inner self at all.

I have noticed that we develop some ways of keeping our radio tuned to the boundaries that other people want. This teaches us how to tune in to others. It does not prepare us to tune in to ourselves and our inner self can become buried.

This buried self makes it hard for us to get the information we need to set our boundaries. You use that information to make every decision, to find your way in every relationship, for your entire life. Boundaries are extremely important for us. I can't go back to my fourth grade teacher and ask her where my boundaries should be now. The boundaries that you need for your decisions and your relationships don't come from the outside. These boundaries come from the inside. I have to figure it out from inside of me and you have to figure it out from inside of you. Before you can do any effective boundary building, you need to get to know your buried self.

I'm going to introduce you to seven people who are each working on building boundaries in their own lives. Each has had to start this boundary work by seeing his or her buried self. Each is struggling with boundaries in relationships to other people, to themselves, and in work or life situations. Their stories are very typical of how we all struggle with our boundaries and lose contact with our inner self. As you read their stories, you may recognize parts of yourself. Think of these seven people as a mosaic.

These people have one thing in common: they all lose touch with their inner voice. They bury themselves by working too much, or shopping too much, or drinking too much, or even helping too much.

As you read this book, follow their stories and notice how each of them learns the essential boundary building skills. Each person applies the skills a little differently, and as you read, you will also be discovering how to apply the skills in your own life.

Wendy, Workaholic

Wendy has a very nice home, a very nice car, and she earns a good paycheck at her job. She always takes work home with her from the office. Sometimes she puts in an extra few hours in the evening on the computer. Certainly on the weekends, there are always just a few more things to get done. Before she goes to bed at night, lists of things she needs to get done at work are dancing through her head. She has figured out that the only way she can get to sleep is to write down a list, next to her bed, of what else she needs to get done tomorrow.

Wendy never feels like her job for the week or job for the day is done. She is grateful to have her work, grateful to earn a good paycheck, but there are times when she realizes that she does not get enough time off. She feels there is too much to do, and if she takes time off, she will fall behind, just making her list longer. Wendy sort of takes vacations, but she finds there are some projects she must bring along and attend to. Of course, she also returns important business calls while on vacation.

Wendy knows she has boundary problems with her work. She does not know how to turn it off. She is not sure she even has an "off" switch.

A tiny voice inside Wendy says, "I am working too much and I don't know how to stop." She is plowing over that tiny voice every day by piling on more to do and more expectations. She covers up her inner voice with "work". Wendy is suffering from workaholism.

Davis, Caretaker

Davis is a counselor who works with the dying at a hospital. His mother had a stroke a year ago and moved in with Davis. Davis and his partner Robert have been trying to adopt a child for years and, frustrated with the system, they became foster parents to a little girl who has many special needs. Robert is a public defender attorney who puts in long hours at the office. Robert often comes home after 7:00 p.m., worn out from the day. The burden of cooking meals, following up with homework, and caring for Nana, his mother, falls to Davis. Davis says all of this gives meaning and purpose to his life. Davis does not complain about his responsibilities, but he does not have time for anything other than taking care of other people. He finds when he goes to the gym, he skips the workout, and prefers to just sit in the sauna. The sauna break provides the only few minutes in the week he has to himself. Davis is becoming worn down. He wakes up tired and he lays down tired. His doctor has said he must lose weight and start exercising as he is at risk for health issues. Davis feels needed by everyone around him and he can't imagine taking any time for himself, even for a walk around the block. He thinks he would be abandoning the people who need him. Sometimes, though, he resents the fact that Robert doesn't cook or help with homework. He sometimes has outbursts, yelling at Robert, but that doesn't seem to result in help with dishes or laundry.

Davis wonders how it ended up this way. He feels depleted and frustrated. Things seem unfair, but he doesn't have any idea how any of it will ever change.

Davis is a caretaker. He has filled up his life meeting the needs of others. Everyone needs him. There is no balance in his life. He can't find time to read a book or to meet any of his own needs. He knows he is loved and appreciated by everyone in his life, but he feels empty inside. It does not seem possible to set boundaries with anyone who needs him, Nana, his daughter, the dying patients, or his exhausted partner.

It is very common for caretakers to find it impossible to ever listen to their inner voice. The people around them are dependent and do need constant assistance. It feels impossible to set boundaries because the needs of others are so high.

Lisa, Sacrificer

Lisa can really relate to Davis. She also has filled up her life taking care of others, but Lisa has a slightly different story. Lisa married her high school sweetheart. They both had dreams of college, but decided that to financially afford school, they would do it one at time. While Lisa worked two jobs waitressing, a daytime job and night job, she paid to put her husband through school. He got one degree and then decided he needed a law degree. Lisa thought she would start college when he finished but since he needed a law degree, she continued to work so they would not be burdened with a high debt from student loans. When her husband finished law school, he got a job and asked her to wait one more year for school to save some money for a new car. After the car was purchased, he wanted her to wait until they had a down payment for a house. Then, he announced that he was no longer in love with her and had met someone who he believed was his soul mate.

Lisa gave up her dream of going to college to support her husband. She sacrificed her inner voice. Lisa is a sacrificer. Sacrificers always believe that someone else's needs are more important than their own. Sacrificers can believe there is a divine or spiritual reason that they should not meet their needs. Sacrificers have a hard time recognizing that their own needs, their voice inside, is important or that it matters.

Sacrificers often hope someone else will sacrifice for them and this often does not happen, leaving Lisa and many others with lives devastated by debt, unfulfilled dreams, and a feeling that years and decades were wasted.

Apply It:

You have just met Wendy, Davis, and Lisa. These are three of our seven people. To figure out if you are a little bit like Wendy, Davis, or Lisa, ask yourself the following questions. Note if you have a little bit of Wendy, Davis or Lisa in you.

1. Am I a workaholic? Do I have trouble sleeping? Is it hard to stop thinking? Am I always working on something? Do I work during my vacations?

2. Am I carrying the world on my shoulders? Am I responsible to take care of others? Am I exhausted? Am I a "fix it" person? Do I have to fix whatever problems I see? Have I ignored some of my own needs to manage all the responsibilities I have caring for someone else? Do I know I don't have anyone to help me with the load?

3. Am I unhappy with my life? Am I living the life I don't want? Have I sacrificed my own dreams for someone else? Am I living the life someone else wants but putting my own wants or desires to the side?

Journal notes:

Journal notes:

Journal notes:

Chapter 3

I can relate to both Wendy and Davis. I can be a workaholic and a caretaker. In fact, at one time in my life, I can honestly say I was a workaholic-caretaker. I actually combined the two and did them at the same time, full time and literally around the clock.

My story

When I was a workaholic caretaker, I had started a homeless youth shelter. I founded a non-profit organization and raised the community support to open a shelter and housing program. We had a small staff, little money and for two years, I worked without a salary. For seven years, I carried a pager on-call all through the night for any emergencies at the teen shelter. I had twin baby girls of my own at the time, too. They were a year old.

I have recovered from this status. I am no longer a workaholic-caretaker. I share this with you because I want you to know that if you see some part of yourself in Wendy, Davis, or Lisa, learning about boundaries will help you recover. It is possible to change.

Just in case you didn't see yourself in Wendy, Davis, or Lisa, I would like you to meet four more people. Perhaps you will find something familiar in their stories.

Jen, Lover

Jen wishes she had a relationship that lasted like Lisa or Davis. Jen just wants someone to love her. She looks for approval from men. She wants to be loved but she finds it hard to stick with relationships. She notices that she tries to please the men she dates and she can't understand why they give her little in return. Jen feels confused around men. She feels lost. She can't hear her own inner voice at all when she is with a man. Jen is certain that if she really were her real self around a man, he would not be interested. She finds she shares little about herself, appearing private and closed off, when really she is afraid that if she revealed herself, he would not like her or love her. Jen wants to be loved by someone else and she has given up loving herself.

Jen is a lover, seeking love and approval outside without ever approving of herself inside. She has interests, but no one to share them with. Jen feels like a chameleon. She changes who she is to fit others. She has found herself tolerating abusive, hurtful relationships without speaking up. She doesn't know where her boundaries are and it feels like she doesn't have any.

Lovers can sometimes lose themselves in hopes of being loved. They aren't sure how love works, but they are certain that they can't really ask for what they need or want.

Stuart, Isolator

Stuart is a bit like Jen. He also really wants to be loved, but he has given up trying and instead has alienated himself to the point of complete aloneness. Stuart lives alone in a three-bedroom house. He never expected to be alone. He works with a small group of people, but he doesn't socialize with this group after work. He doesn't even eat lunch with them. Stuart has become an isolator. He doesn't trust that reaching out to someone is worthwhile. But Stu is frequently alone and his inner self feels lonely. He does not know how to take down the boundaries that have walled him in.

He has joined a meditation group, but the group sits in long silences, extending Stu's isolation. Stu wants to change and break free of his isolation, but he doesn't know how.

Raven, Numb-er

Raven is also lonely on the inside, but she is not really aware of it. She goes out every weekend. She likes going out to drink, and often drinks to the point of not remembering what happened. She also likes to shop on weekends and has the credit card bills to prove it. Raven numbs her inner self. She drinks and shops to numb out and not deal with her inner voice. Raven appears happy and well put together until she gets drunk. Then, she kind of comes apart. She had a dark, abusive father growing up. She had beatings and damage that she still remembers. Raven feels that she deserves nice clothes and shoes, even if she can't afford them. Raven feels happy when she is drinking; it helps her forget the pain that haunts her from the past. She escapes when she is shopping or drinking. Raven has no idea how to heal the past. She can't change what happened, right? New situations that hurt her are treated the same way, with alcohol and shopping.

She is a numb-er. Numbing affects her boundaries because she doesn't know what she really needs. She doesn't know how to take care of her feelings. She drowns out her inner voice and she can't hear it.

Other ways to numb out are watching too much television, gambling, prescription medication abuse, or even driving in circles without a destination. Numbing can be achieved in many ways.

Maggie, Protector

Maggie is 62. She has been married to Len for 40 years. Len is addicted to pain pills. Maggie absolutely does not see that Len is a drug addict. Len often goes to the doctor for "back pain" and gets prescriptions. Maggie does see that Len is completely out of it in his chair by the TV every night, but she thinks he is just tired from working all day. Len does have a bad back, after all, and it is worse from the three car accidents he has had in the last two years.

Len's grown children are terrified that he is going to die in a car accident high on pain medications. Maggie does not understand what they are worried about. Maggie believes Len needs this medication and it actually makes him easier to get along with. She finds he is more pleasant and less argumentative if he has his medication. Maggie does not believe the narcotics affect his driving one bit. She thinks he probably just needs new glasses.

Maggie is a protector and does not see the truth about her husband. She is afraid to hear the truth. Maggie focuses on protecting her husband and herself from facing the truth about his addiction. Maggie distorts her own inner voice and no longer knows how to hear her truth. When Maggie protects herself by distorting the truth, she distorts herself, too. She can't set useful boundaries because she distorts what she hears inside.

These seven people, Maggie, Lisa, Davis, Jen, Raven, Stuart and Wendy, have normal difficulties. You don't know much about them, but you are learning something about how they have all buried their inner self. We are all a little bit like them.

Apply It:
Before you go any further ahead in this book, take some time to reflect and figure out exactly how you bury your inner self. We are each a little bit like Jen, Stu, Maggie, Davis, Raven, Lisa, and Wendy.

Here are some questions for you to ask yourself:
1. What do I use to numb myself? Television or computer? Alcohol? Pain medication? Driving in circles?

2. I like being alone sometimes, but am I alone all the time? Am I alone to the point that I feel too alone and isolated? Do I

feel like it is too much effort to make a plan with other people? Have I given up on having close relationships?

3. Do I live with someone who has a serious drug problem or a serious mental health problem? Is that person getting help? Am I taking care of them, providing the food, paying the bills, because they can't manage their responsibilities?

4. Am I longing for love? Even when I am in a relationship does it seems like the person doesn't really love me? Does it feel like I'm always the giver in the relationship and the other person is the taker? I love plenty, but I don't see much in return.

Journal notes:

Journal notes:

Journal notes:

Chapter 4

If you set out to build a house, you need to work with materials that you can build a house with, such as bricks, wood, mud, or straw. If you tried to build a house out of water, it would be impossible.

To have boundaries, you need to work with the right material. You need to know exactly what boundaries are made of in order to build them.

Boundaries are made of Yes and No.
Yes and No comes from inside of you.

Yes and No is a voice deep inside of you, and it never goes away. I have watched people do incredibly destructive things to their inner voice, and it does not go away. We can make it hard to hear that inner voice.

Often, when people do hear that inner voice, they struggle or resist. They ignore it because they don't want to do what it tells them. When my inner voice tells me I am working too much, I can be too interested in my work project to listen. I ignore the message. Before you can set boundaries in your life and with other people, you need to be able to listen to this guidance from inside. Listen to your true Yes or No.

When we are too busy working, sacrificing, or protecting other people, we can't really tune in and hear our own inner voice. We are too busy caretaking, working, fixing, isolating, etc.

The changes people make in their lives to really work on their boundaries are part of a process that involves listening to yourself and increasing your self-awareness. People don't just snap their fingers and change their lives. There is no pill you can take to make it easier to negotiate with your partners, your job, and other things.

It may sound overwhelming to make the changes that Davis, Wendy, and you will be making. The truth is that living without boundaries is what is actually overwhelming you. Being a workaholic is overwhelming. Sacrificing is overwhelming. The things you are doing all the time are not actually making your boundaries better. These behaviors, the way you bury your inner self and ignore your own needs, are the first places where you begin to dig out your real Yes and No. You begin by listening to that tiny voice inside that knows you have needs. Learning to listen to your Yes and No is a process and it requires constant attention to stay aware of what is true for you.

Let's look at Wendy and how her inner voice is still trying to get her to notice that she is working too much. Wendy knows she is working too much. She is not in denial about this. She can even hear a "tiny itty bitty" voice inside saying, "This is too much." Her voice feels tiny because that is what happens to our Yes and No when we don't listen to it. Rather than being strong and big and clear, it feels tiny and powerless.

Many of us do exactly what Wendy does. After we make our inner Yes and No feel tiny and powerless, we run around scratching our heads, wondering why it is hard for us to set boundaries!

Wendy feels like she can't work less. What do you think Wendy would need to do to empower that "little" voice and make it stronger? You guessed it. She would need to listen to it, but she doesn't. She continues working.

The key to her recovery is that she must listen to the little voice. Wendy begins by asking her little voice, when should I stop? Wendy makes a deal with her inner voice and she sets a time when she will step away from her work no matter what, every day. She is taking her first step by making a deal to listen at least once each day, at quitting time.

I will tell you that listening to yourself once a day is really just a start. It is not enough to really establish the awareness needed for your boundaries. This work has to have a starting point though, and for Wendy it is one time each day.

When we begin to listen to our inner Yes and No, we are starting a relationship with ourselves that is brand new. Wendy is learning that there is something inside of her that knows what she needs.

Wendy is working so much because it makes her feel successful and helps her avoid facing some things that she doesn't want to share yet about her life. Wendy is a bit like Raven. Wendy covers things up with working, and Raven covers things up with drinking.

Raven is also drowning out the little voice inside of her. Raven's relationship with her inner Yes and No is being distorted. When Raven drinks, she finds herself doing things she would never, ever do when sober. Raven is not really as loud and daring as she appears. She only seems this way when she drinks. Raven is twisting her Yes and No like a contortionist. Raven has to get sober to hear her Yes and No accurately. She's become confused by some of the choices she made while drinking. She is not really sure about which reality is hers, the one she made while drinking or the one she thinks about when she is not drinking? It's like she is waking up and can't quite figure out where home is. She has lost her connection with her inner voice and she is not able to trust herself. Her Yes and No inside are very far from her and she can't really hear them clearly like Wendy does. This is normal for people recovering from addiction and also from domestic violence. It is going to take more time to restore a connection to a true Yes and No.

We erode trust when we don't listen to our own Yes and No. Raven's drinking made her lose trust in herself. She did many things while drunk that were not safe or good for her and now her inner self is withdrawn from her.

Davis is not sure any of this applies to his own life. He feels like he can't change. He thinks Wendy and Raven have it a little easier because they can choose to change. Raven stopped drinking and Wendy can work less. Davis doesn't have a choice. Davis has people who need him. His daughter needs homework help, food cooked, clothes washed, love and attention. His mother needs meals, exercise, someone to talk to, her hair brushed, her clothes washed, doctor appointments. It would be much easier for Davis if his partner Robert helped, but Robert does not help and Davis does not ask for help.

Davis's health is at risk from not taking care of himself. He is committed to doing this work and can't just watch the other seven people learn the boundaries. Watching will not help him.

I have given Davis an assignment: to select one of his own needs and make the time for it.

Davis misses reading books. He begins by taking a baby step to make some reading time. He will request that Robert help out with one thing each night to give himself time. This reading time will be scheduled so that Davis keeps his commitment to himself. Davis puts a list on the fridge to note his reading time daily. He will need to read in the privacy of his bedroom with a sign on the door that says, "No interruptions for 40 minutes." It will take a great deal of effort for Davis to make time for himself. He will have to protect this time. It will not meet all of Davis's needs, but it is a first step. It is a big step.

If you take steps to listen to your Yes and No, things will get much, much better and the feeling of being overwhelmed will disappear. One day, you will wake up and realize you are listening to your Yes and No and you are no longer overwhelmed.

Listening to Yes and No, listening to your boundaries, will save you from workaholism, caretaking, sacrificing, numbing yourself, and isolation.

In small reasonable doses, working, helping, escaping reality, or having alone time are not hurting you. But living in these places full-time, or swinging from one to another and another, leaves us disconnected from ourselves.

Apply It:
In the last chapter, you indicated the behaviors you relate to. Circle those again here: Workaholism, Caretaking, Sacrificing, Numbing, Protecting, Isolation, Lover.

Inside you, you have a voice, a Yes and No, trying to tell you something. This tiny voice is your wisdom. It is going to help you. How does this voice help you? What is it saying?

Davis had an "I can't" story and many of us come up with reasons why we can't.

What has been your "I can't" story?

Journal notes:

Journal notes:

Journal notes:

Chapter 5

The whole purpose of our boundaries, our inner Yes and No, is to take care of us. When we do not allow our boundaries to take care of us, we will pay a high price.

Sometimes we argue with our boundaries, mostly because we are trying to take care of other people. We don't want to do what our inner voice of Yes and No says to take care of ourselves. We argue, fight, or ignore our inner Yes and No.

Your inner Yes and No have one purpose, to take care of you.

A high price is paid for not allowing your boundaries to take care of you. I paid this price when I was a workaholic-caretaker. You pay a price too.

The inner spirit, trying to take care of us, can see that it is being ignored. We suffer when we are ignoring this part of ourselves. I think of it as the inner spirit or soul. A suffering soul gets symptoms. Each person gets his own kind of symptoms. The symptoms may be depression, inability to sleep, feeling like running away, drinking/numbing ourselves, doing high-risk behavior, feeling like a spinning top, getting headaches or body pain. The spirit/soul expresses this suffering in many ways.

Many people would like to treat the symptoms of suffering inside with medication or pills. The symptoms of depression or frustration or sleeplessness can become large and we start tricking ourselves into thinking that the depression or sleeplessness is the problem. As a therapist, when I hear someone describe symptoms like these, I believe the depression and sleeplessness is actually trying to help the person. I believe the depression is trying to save you. When we ignore listening to our own truth, our own wise Yes and No, the spirit turns on body signals. Something we can't ignore. Something we will notice.

Depression, sleeplessness, and frustration all have strong connections to our Yes and No. But many people want to ignore that noise and take a pill to make it go away. They still don't really want to listen.

To be clear, I don't believe all depression comes from a problem with Yes and No. Many things can trigger these symptoms, including chemistry issues and brain functioning, life issues and trauma. I am only stating that ignoring your inner Yes and No is also a way to trigger depression.

If there is a problem with listening to Yes and No, problems with setting boundaries, there is no pill that will fix it. We can use medication to help your brain with the symptoms of depression, but it is always essential to figure out what is triggering the symptoms. If self-care is a problem, if boundaries are a struggle, these skills can be learned. Learning skills to self-manage, to set boundaries, will help you take care of yourself. It can feel a bit overwhelming to really learn how to listen to your Yes and No. For some people it can feel too hard. If it feels too hard, that is an "I can't" story.

Listening to yourself is difficult. But which difficulty would you prefer, the difficulties of living without boundaries or the difficulty of learning the skills to have boundaries?

Lisa sacrificed her own education, her own dreams, to take care of her husband. Her husband has his own inner Yes and No. He can take care of his own needs, which he did. He did not really need Lisa to sacrifice herself. She made the sacrifice, waiting for him to do the same one day. This is a terrible way to get your needs met in the world.

Many people come to therapy disappointed that their relationships never fulfilled their needs. One big reason for some of the disappointment is that we are required to be sure we are fulfilling our own needs. Most of the time, people have outsourced that, hoping someone else will meet their needs.

In partnerships/marriages, we have different roles in how we support each other to meet our needs and in what we give to each other. It is hard to recognize if we have enough of our energy to support and nurture each other while at the same time nurturing ourselves, too.

Lisa is typical of many people who find themselves sacrificing what they need, giving to the point of inner bankruptcy, for the love of someone else.

Maggie, Stu, and Jen have also paid a big price for caretaking, love, and protecting. Maggie, protecting her addicted husband, has sacrificed all of her relationships. People don't want to spend time with her because she covers up the truth that everyone else can see. When she makes excuses about her husband's behavior, people wonder what else she lies about. They don't understand that she is trying to protect him. Her grown kids certainly don't understand it. They avoid going home completely. The price Maggie pays is that she feels alone inside, without her family and friends, but she also feels alone around her husband. He is not really present. Worst of all, she feels disconnected from herself. She feels lost inside. She feels lost in the same way that Raven, who numbs herself, feels lost. She feels alone the way Stu does. Stu actually lives alone, and he expects to be lonely, but Maggie lives with her husband and feels as lonely as Stu.

Jen is hungry for love, and she finds herself settling for very little. Relationship does not mean love. Jen settles for relationships that are less than what she really wants. The more she makes herself a chameleon to fit any man she meets, the more she loses of herself. She doesn't really love herself inside. She blames herself for not being loved, never thinking that when she chooses someone, she gives up all of her boundaries. Without boundaries to take care of her, she finds herself terribly abused in relationships. In fact, when we do not have our boundaries in the right place, when we do not allow our boundaries to take care of us, we often get to a point of exhaustion, depletion, and feeling used and taken for granted by others.

Stuart is isolated and his whole body has aches and pains. He makes appointments to go to the doctor, but they can't find anything to treat. He tries a naturopath, changes his diet. When he talks, I notice he has continuous negative, hopeless thinking. His words are the words of depression talking.

Stuart wasn't aware that he had slipped into depression. Stuart thought depressed people cry a lot or feel suicidal. It is completely normal for people to miss the signs of depression in themselves. Stuart's depression makes him think recovery isn't possible. He doesn't believe he can ever feel better. Stuart is paying a big price for his isolation and he is going to need to listen to his true Yes and No to help him recover. His inner Yes and No know exactly what he needs to recover, but he needs to listen and trust this wisdom from inside.

Apply It:

Think about the price you are paying for your workaholism, isolation, protection, caretaking, need to be loved, numbing, sacrificing.

What is the price? What are the consequences for you?

Whenever you feel like this boundary work is too hard, I want you to go to this page in your journal and remember the price you pay, the ways you suffer, to help keep you moving through choosing your self-care.

Journal notes:

Journal notes:

Journal notes:

Chapter 6

It is normal to find self-care confusing and even impossible. It takes a great amount of reflection, listening to our inner voice, and learning about things that are nourishing to our mind, body, and spirit. Every person has self-care needs. Some self-care needs are specific to you, such as the passion you may find doing artwork, or the peace you find walking in the woods. Other self-care needs are more generic and are good for everyone, such as eating healthy food, exercising, and keeping your brain challenged.

I am often asked, "How much self-care do I need?" It all depends on how you want to feel. Think about how you want to feel going through your day to day to life. Do you want to feel energized, creative, passionate and joyful? Do you want to feel numb, sad, anxious, drained or overwhelmed with tasks?

You need to watch and observe yourself. Study yourself to recognize what makes you feel good, what makes you feel great, what gives you peace. How much of that would you actually like to experience? As we begin to take our first step setting our first boundary, we begin a journey. We are traveling down a new road, and for the first time, there are options that we've never seen before. We can make new choices. Rather than choices that overwhelm and drain us, we can keep choosing self-care. Many more opportunities to improve your self-care are ahead for you and for the first time in your life, you will recognize those opportunities and you will dare to take them. Each time you do, you will expand your self-care and you will feel better and better and better.

Self-care is a practice. It is something you choose to do, not something that happens to you all at once. You have to keep selecting self-care in order to have self-care.

I would love to eat chocolate cake every day. Sometimes, I choose the cake. Most days though, I choose fresh fruit instead. I have to choose. The same is true with all of self-care. It is not automatically selected. We must choose it every single day.

As I worked on my own self-care, I observed that I had a need and deep enjoyment of being in quiet. I thought my interest in quiet would be met in a Buddhist silent retreat setting. But interestingly, I did not find that sitting quietly in meditation to be the kind of quiet my spirit was seeking. I felt too restricted. I discovered that I liked moving about and being or working in quiet spaces. I liked phones off, music off, a private room. I realized that even when seeing clients, I liked the entire office building to be quiet. The more quiet I experienced, such as having the radio off in my car, the more my spirit liked it. Finding out what I meant by "quiet" took a bit of experimentation. I rearranged some things in my house to have quieter spaces. The journey to my self-care need for quiet took lots of twists and turns. Some worked and some didn't, but I learned about myself and what I needed to create the quiet that worked for me.

My self-care also includes knitting daily. I find joy in the artful colors, making knitted gifts for loved ones, learning new knitting skills, and shopping for yarn. I find joy in every part of knitting. It makes me happy. It also feels like praying. I knit and think of the person I am knitting for in a meditative sort of way.

Each person needs to create a daily self-care plan. This plan will change as you get to know yourself better. I've added reading breaks all through my day as part of my self-care. I take time to stop and breathe. The breathing is appreciating letting myself "be" without "doing". It is non-doing time. Just be. I have a high value on remembering to "be". It helps to intervene on my workaholism.

Self-care plan means you write out an actual plan that you follow, the same way you follow the other commitments you put on your calendar. If you don't make a plan with yourself, it becomes harder to do.

We all come to self-care at different starting points.

Davis has a question. "Isn't it selfish to meet your own needs? That just seems incredibly selfish and self-focused."

Davis, here is my answer. After decades of being a therapist, experiencing many people, I have noticed something. People who struggle with boundaries are never selfish. They are not self-focused at all. People who struggle with boundaries tend to be highly sensitive to others. They are extremely observant and aware of the needs of others.

Selfish people lack the awareness of others. Selfish people are not sensitive to others, and they seem unaware of how others feel. The people who attend my workshops, and people who are reading this book, suffer from high sensitivity and awareness of others. You will never lose that awareness of others. You will learn how to make different choices in the presence of all that you are aware of.

Now, you will also pay attention to an awareness of yourself. You will stop avoiding and drowning out an awareness of you.

Raven, who has used drinking, shopping, and anything that will numb her out, realizes that her first step toward listening to herself is to stop drinking. She is terrified, thinking of her life without drinking, but she has realized that she is drowning out her inner voice inside, her Yes and No. Raven understands that she can't do numbing things because it silences her on the inside.

Deep inside, she is sure she doesn't like her inner self and is terrified because she knows when she stops numbing herself, she will have to face how she feels about herself. This is what she dreads.

I remind Raven that her boundaries will help her through this, too. Her boundaries will help her with self-care. All of the self-loathing can heal in time as she learns how to truly care for self. The emphasis will be to learn the caring skills for this inside self-loathing.

There really isn't any other way to deal with self-loathing. For Raven to eventually feel better and recover from the things that were crushing to her, she has to learn how to truly care for the crushed parts of herself. She has to take care of the brokenness. Drinking will never do that. Shopping will never do that. Numbing will never do that. The numbing will silence it, but it sits there, unchanged, unhealed, always hurting.

I don't want Raven to expect to feel better right away. She can really take pride in getting the boundary with alcohol, but behind the boundary, there is a big clean up job. There is a big self-care job and she has to learn how to do this. It isn't easy.

Apply it:
Create a list of the self-care things you forget, ignore, or don't get to.

Include everything from eating well, making your dentist appointment, to the enjoyable things that you don't have time for. This should be a long list.

Journal notes:

Journal notes:

Journal notes:

Chapter 7

Figuring out your self-care needs is a process. You need a daily self-care plan. Writing a plan is challenging and you will find yourself resisting writing a plan. You will find that writing it helps you figure out your commitment.

Your plan will be personal and specific to fit only you. Self-care plans develop over time and you will find that over time your commitments to your care will become stronger.

For Davis, who has been taking care of many people, it will take a few years, one step at a time, before he can say his life feels balanced. By balanced, I mean he will no longer have symptoms from ignoring his self-care. I don't want you to feel hopeless hearing how long it will take. I want to be honest. It won't take everyone years. The amount of time this takes depends on how far you have gone with workaholism, caregiving, isolating, loving, numbing, sacrificing, or protecting.

Our bodies give us signals and symptoms when we ignore our self-care.

I used to be the type of person who got in the car and went to work when I was sick. Fever, coughing, sneezing, didn't matter. I didn't matter. Now, I would never ever do that. I understand that when I am sick, I must stop, rest, and recover. I don't fight with my body and push on. I listen. Of course I don't want to stay down in bed, but I do. I am committed to my self-care and my well-being. I have also become aware that no one else wants to be exposed to my sickness. It is not OK to spread my cold around. It is also never OK for me to treat myself like I don't matter.

Resisting or ignoring our body signals has consequences for us. Our bodies are part of our compass, our wisdom. If we truly want to be wise, we need to listen to what our body tells us.

Davis takes one step at a time. He has Robert helping with dinners and even taking over dinner. He divides homework nights with his partner and realizes that grandmother can be a good listener to the nightly reading with his daughter. Davis was so busy in his caretaking role, he stopped noticing that the people around him did have certain abilities. Each person in the household can contribute to take care of the responsibilities.

Davis picked one night a week to be at the gym. He loved having a night "off." He felt guilty at first and it was hard to leave the house, but once he got to the gym, he enjoyed the time. He yearned for a night out to go the movies. He decided one night to sneak off to the movies instead of the gym. He liked this and he decided that once a month he would use gym time for a movie. Davis realized that his pleasures were not harming anyone. Sure, some nights his partner brought take-out instead of cooking, but so what? His daughter actually preferred reading aloud to Grandma because Grandma smiled and enjoyed listening and didn't correct her mistakes. Grandma enjoyed being read to. It wasn't a chore to her at all. Davis recognized that he was much happier the day after his one night "off" than he was all week. He realized that this happiness was something his family loved to see. It was a big realization to Davis that his happiness level was more important to his family, more appreciated by his family than all the chores he did. They didn't really care if the dishes were clean but he was annoyed. It was more important to them that he was happy when reading a novel after dinner and letting the dishes wait.

We can become robotic about our tasks, our things we must do and forget about how we are feeling. Davis realized that much of the time while doing all the things he did, he was in robot mode. He wasn't happy or sad. He wasn't able to know what he was feeling. He just knew he had more things to do as soon as he finished whatever he was doing. He was numb.

On his night off, Davis was not numb. His feelings returned. Noticing numbness is a good way to tell that we need to stop what we are doing, and do self-care.

I do self-care all through the day. I am not letting myself go numb. I am staying connected to my joy, connected to my well-being, by doing self-care all through the day. I still work. I work plenty in fact. But I plan my work around my self-care rather than planning my self-care around my work. I will admit that this is a hard-earned achievement and took years to accomplish. It is like being a marathon runner. No one starts out day one of running by going 26 miles. You begin slowly and keep increasing. The same is true with self-care. You increase until you achieve the balance point for yourself.

Wendy has been completely consumed with her work. She realizes that waiting for work to have a "calm time" isn't really setting a boundary of her own. She has been waiting for work to set the boundary for her. She has waited for the email to slow down, for the projects to wrap up, and for her once-a-year vacation. She is not setting boundaries from inside. I give her an assignment to track her working hours daily. Wendy counts her hours, including her working lunches eating her sandwich in front of her computer or sipping soup while on the phone. She realizes that her days are 14 working hours, five days a week, plus a couple of hours on the weekend. She is working close to 70 or 75 hours per week. She is paid for 40. There are 168 hours in a week. Wendy doesn't get extra hours for trying harder or earning more money. We each have 168 hours weekly. Forty-nine hours are set aside for sleep, leaving 119 hours for everything else. Wendy uses 70-75 hours for work, leaving her little time for the rest of her life. As Wendy thinks about how she crams nearly two work weeks into one week, and donates 30-35 hours of pay along with it, she understands that she must make some changes.

She doesn't really have ideas about what else she might want to do, but she understands that she has not been offering herself the time to develop other interests. Whatever other interests Wendy might have are in "storage" inside of her. It is dark in the storage area, and she will need to give her interests some time living in broad daylight before these interests will emerge. They will surprise her.

Since Wendy's work is not going to slow down, she is going to need some strategies to protect her time from work. She will need to set boundaries with how often she checks her computer and phone for work messages. She needs to set specific work hours and then make herself stop. As she tries to set up strategies, she will also need to evaluate how much work she can take on at one time and manage well. Wendy works at a high performance level, demanding quality, accuracy, and excellence. When she works at overload, she is distraught trying to maintain that quality, accuracy, and excellence. The more she overloads herself with work, the more she struggles to maintain her high standard. Cutting down her work hours and her work load will allow her to maintain her quality, accuracy, and excellence. She has to create a strategy to bring her work into a reasonable load of a 40-hour work week. She can't passively wait and just hope in a year her load will diminish. Waiting for her workload to diminish does not give Wendy the practice she needs setting boundaries.

Boundary setting is an active process. It does require taking steps. Sometimes taking the steps to make a boundary happen can make us afraid. It may mean other people may not get everything they want or need or expect from us. Wendy is setting a boundary about her work and that means she won't be responding to emails and phone calls during her off hours. It means that while other people are not getting what they want from Wendy, Wendy is getting what she needs with herself. It means Wendy is finally going to take the 7 p.m. yoga class three nights per week.

Wendy made a great first step by committing to this yoga class. Her phone would not be welcome in class. It will also give her time to "let go" of her work, and connect with her own body, her own breathing.

She is scared to turn away from her phone for the yoga class. Her fear is similar to Raven's fear when Raven stepped away from alcohol. Raven is terrified to face her self-loathing, and she is certain it will pounce upon her every chance it gets.

Raven discovered there were moments of despair, but there was something new, moments of genuine cheering for herself as she went day after day without drinking.

Wendy is afraid to separate from her phone but at the end of her first yoga class, she finds that she doesn't feel scared. She feels peaceful and calm. This surprised her. The fear, for that evening, was gone.

Apply it:

Take the list you completed in the previous chapter of your self-care needs and now make an actual self-care plan. This means figuring out when you will do the things on your list. Take out your calendar and block out the time you will do your self-care activities. The time you devote is a commitment. You may find that your self-care involves signing up for a class or joining a book club. Decide how, when, and where you will follow through.

Be sure that every single day has at least one to three self-care things each day for you. If you try something and it is not filling your soul, scratch it off your list and find something else. It will take some time trying out different things to discover what works for you.

Journal notes:

Journal notes:

Journal notes:

Chapter 8

Establishing true self-care is required to do any boundary work in your life. Self-care is a relationship with your soul. This is a significant and sacred commitment, to listen to your soul.

Stuart is thinking he'd like to go to the gym to begin breaking his isolation. He can buy a month-to-month membership or a one-year membership. He thinks if he buys the yearly membership, it will force him to go to the gym. This is not accurate. The membership will not require anything of Stuart. Stuart has to rally himself to go to the gym. The truth is that he doesn't trust himself to follow up and use it. I encourage Stuart to listen to his soul not trusting him. I explain that ignoring that voice in side of him would not be helpful. Stuart needs to show his soul that he can hear it. He buys a month-to-month membership.

The trust between our own souls and ourselves is earned by our actions. Stuart will go to the gym realizing that it is not only to break some of his isolation but also because he needs to earn trust with his inner self. Trust and confidence in your self-care is earned one hour at a time, one day at a time, one week, one month, three months, year by year. Stuart will build trust and self-care by earning it.

Maggie also has to unearth herself from decades of not paying attention to herself. She has been isolated in her marriage and her home as her husband Len has slipped into pain medication addiction and drinking.

Maggie begins her self-care by taking walks. She walks on the road in front of her house. She wants Len to go with her, but he won't. It is hard for her to go out each day for walks without Len, but it is the only thing she could list on her self-care list. She understands she must start with herself. She still wants to care for Len and have him come with her, but the truth is that Maggie's self-care isn't exactly what Len needs. If she could really get Len to do self-care he would need other things.

Maggie keeps her commitment, even on days when it is raining. She goes outside and walks. Then she thinks, why not take walks on other roads? She explores her community by foot, creating new routes to try out each week. The more she walks, the more she wants to move. She notices an advertisement for a Tai Chi class and decides to give it a try. From there, she notices a longing for a bicycle and now that she is excited to hear this from her inner voice, she purchases a bicycle. Maggie has never ridden a bicycle. It was always a fantasy, a bike with a basket. She finds joy in going everywhere by bike. She buys herself some jeans and a good jacket for riding. Maggie and her bike go to the Saturday farmers market for groceries, the library for books, and once a week, a bike meet-up with the senior center where she had been taking the Tai Chi class.

Maggie has left her sad and dreary living room, watching her husband zoned out in front of the television. She is outside, riding, laughing, enjoying the beauty she sees everywhere. As Maggie begins to enjoy the outside, she notices that as she returns home from her rides, sadness begins to move in. At first, Maggie thought the sadness was because the ride was ending. But the more she reflected, the more she realized that she didn't like being at home. She didn't feel at home there.

The more Maggie follows through and does her self-care, the more her self-care interests grow. She has established trust with her inner self and this is why she can hear this inner voice telling her to get a bicycle. Her inner self will tell her more things and Maggie is learning how to listen to this wisdom from within. This guidance will be required for her to set boundaries in the future.

Maggie, Stuart, Wendy, and all of us can have a hard time setting boundaries when we don't have a connection to our own self. This connection to the self is necessary.

Jen has been spending her last fifteen years trying to establish connection to someone else. She has not thought at all that the person she needed a connection to was herself. She has been a chameleon trying to fit in to a man's life. She has been pursuing a relationship to someone else.

When Jen tried to write a self-care list, she couldn't come up with anything. This can happen. Sometimes we can feel far away from our real self. We can feel cut off and unable to know what we need. Jen feels depressed and worried that other people can come up with ideas and she is not able to. I ask her to have the depression write her a letter. Let the depression tell you why it feels this way and what it needs from you.

Jen didn't want to do the assignment and sit with this miserable feeling. But it is where her real self is. Her inside self is engulfed in feeling depressed and hopeless.

In the letter, Jen learns this depressed feeling doesn't think anything is going to work. It has watched Jen try everything to find a boyfriend and nothing has worked. It tells her she doesn't know what she needs because she never listens to this inside voice. She is only looking for someone outside. It is like she is not really good enough.

Jen is heartbroken when she reads this letter. She has learned that she has told herself that she is not good enough. She understands why she is having such a hard time. I explain to her that she needs to begin her self-care by taking care of the wounded, hurt part inside of herself. She needs to stop living like she is not good enough.

I ask Jen to create a list of ways she can encourage herself. Jen returns with an interesting list. She has made a list of the top three things she has wanted to learn to do. She has enrolled in classes and bought books to begin learning the things on her list.

Jen has always wanted to learn to rock climb, cook, and speak Spanish. She explains that she will be encouraging herself by doing new things. She will be literally encouraging herself with every step on her path. She isn't too concerned about how great of a cook she becomes, rather, she sees these as her sandbox. They are ways to practice encouraging herself.

Apply it:
Look at your own self-care plan. How do you earn trust with yourself in your own plan?

What ways will prove to yourself that you are doing your self-care?

Building a connection to yourself and trusting that connection is the foundation of boundaries.

How much time each day are you spending staying connected to you? Are you eating enough? Staying hydrated? Taking breaks when you need to? Going to the bathroom when you need to? Your body gives you signals all day long. Are you listening?

Journal notes:

Journal notes:

Journal notes:

Chapter 9

I want to give you realistic expectations about doing boundary work and the self-care that is part of it. Boundaries have one job, to take care of you. Self-care is the most important thing you can focus on if you are going to improve your boundaries. Self-care is something that we must keep our attention on and if we take our attention off of it, things can get messy in our lives. We can see ourselves sliding backwards. We recognize the familiar feelings of being overwhelmed, exhausted, too much on our plate, no time for ourselves. Our symptoms return, like a virus. We catch it again! We can find ourselves doing well setting boundaries with one person or in one place in our lives and we can still be struggling in another place in our lives.

Boundary setting is ongoing work. We keep doing it. It comes up again and again, throughout our whole life. We'll talk more about boundaries in later chapters, but self-care is the foundation of any boundary work and we must keep our attention on our self-care because that is something that changes as we live. Our self-care needs can change.

Jen wants to know how she will know she has finished with her boundary work.

Do not look for the finish line with boundary work. It is about staying present and healthy and focused on recognizing when you need to set a boundary. It can come up at any time. It can come up any place. It can come up with any person. It is your job to pay attention and set your boundary when it is needed.

Maggie sees her big challenge as her husband Len, and he is her biggest challenge for now. There are also other people in Maggie's life and she will need to be ready to say Yes and No to plenty of things when it comes to the other people in her life, too.

We have tendencies that we are drawn toward. Wendy and Lisa will both always be drawn to work harder, try harder, and sacrifice more. Davis will always feel as if he should take care of someone. Wendy, Lisa, and Davis will learn to call this their "first response". I have noticed that our "first response" doesn't ever fully extinguish. When Raven gets overwhelmed, she will always want to escape. Escaping will be Raven's "first response". She will learn to never choose her first response. She will learn to live with the mode, but not act on it. It will come up, when Raven has a bad day, an expensive traffic ticket, or a problem she can't solve, she will want to escape her feelings and numb out. She won't drink, though. She now has a boundary on this mode. She will recognize the feeling of wanting to escape and she will say to herself, that is just my "first response". I am going to skip that response and go to the response I choose instead. Learning to ignore her first response will give Raven more options when she is confronting problems.

We can become an expert at setting boundaries. We can truly become masters of this, but the problems, the challenges to our boundaries will never go away. We will simply be armed with a better way to respond. We will respond in a way that allows us to take care of ourselves. That is what all this self-care stuff is about.

Lisa is used to taking care of someone else first. As a result, no one is taking care of Lisa. She will learn that she can't abandon herself. She may think she "should" take care of someone else, but Lisa is learning to stop and ask herself some questions first. Lisa has come up with two questions:

1) Is it my job or their job to take care of their wants, needs, desires?
2) Do I have a need or desire of my own that I could work on?

Lisa uses these two questions as a way to remind herself about not stepping over her own boundary.

Wendy wishes she could use questions to stop herself from working but that doesn't seem to work for her. Wendy has to preset alarms around her desk. Literally, she sets them for a lunch break and she sets them to go home. She also has found it helps to make plans in the middle of the week on Wednesday night. Her work starts to build up as the week goes on and she will stay late at work if she doesn't have a plan. But she has signed up for a yoga class on Wednesday nights to force her out of her office. Wendy can't believe how hard it is for her to pull away from her desk. She is committed to it. She just wants to know when it will get easier.

Easier?
Did I ever say boundary work is easy?

I have watched people struggle with it for a long time. Some people struggle for six months, and each time they say no, each time they set a boundary, it is truly hard won. I have watched other people wrestle with boundary setting for 15 months, and each and every time they fight with saying no, each boundary is fraught with tears and angst for them.

But then, something happens. There is a breakthrough. The breakthrough happens when they are not fighting over the no, they are not arguing with themselves, feeling guilty, and wishing they didn't have to set a boundary. The breakthrough comes when they are cheering for themselves, encouraging themselves to set a boundary, and wanting to set the boundary. Once they have a breakthrough, they want to take care of themselves. They see it as a priority. They are grateful to see the light.

That is the big win. The boundary work hasn't actually gone away. They haven't solved it. The big a-ha moment, the big breakthrough, is they are not struggling over saying no. Lisa, Wendy, Davis, and Raven want to take care of themselves. That is their big breakthrough. They want to get past their first response and choose their actual response.

Lisa has one thing on her self-care list: go to college. Lisa doesn't know where the money will come from. She will get some money in her divorce settlement, but the payments will not be enough to cover everything she needs for school. She isn't sure she should go to school. She doesn't believe she can afford it. But she knows this is part of her self-care.

Apply it:

We can each think of hurdles, struggles, first responses, things we must overcome if we are going to do self-care. I can always find more work to do rather than do my self-care.

What is your hurdle? Make a list of the ways doing self-care is hard for you. Know your obstacles.

The challenge is not allowing them to be obstacles any longer. What will you need to overcome?

Journal notes:

Journal notes:

Journal notes:

Chapter 10

As we each develop a better connection to our inner Yes and No regarding our self-care, we can find ourselves standing in a new and unfamiliar place. I call it the "Now-what?" place.

Our inner Yes and No don't necessarily make the plan for us. They don't hold a map for us. We can hear our Yes and No, but we may not have ourselves organized with a plan.

People are planners. We have career plans, family plans, holiday plans, summer plans and school plans. We have plans for everything. It can be difficult to listen to your inner guidance, your Yes and No, because it doesn't have a plan. In my therapy room, I have listened to many people with a sure sense of what is a Yes and No for them, but they don't listen to their Yes or No because the Yes or No doesn't have a plan. After you do the hard work of connecting to your Yes and No, you have to accept the answer without a plan! This is difficult for people. You make the plan and you live your way into the plan as you go along.

As Maggie pursues bike rides, painting class, and walks outside, she hears a voice inside of her that no longer wants to return home to her husband who is overmedicated and zoned out in front of the television all evening. Maggie used to be isolated at home and was certain this was her destiny. As she began to listen to her inner voice, it guided her away from the troubling, lonely house and her husband who had a drug and alcohol problem. Maggie never imagined that there was a part of her that really didn't want to live with her husband any longer. She always thought she knew exactly what her life looked like. At first, she thought she was too old to change her life.

She didn't have a plan and she didn't know how she would manage financially. She didn't even know where she wanted to live. She only knew that her real voice, her soul, was saying her husband was no longer her home. Even though she knew all this for sure, she was filled with doubt. She didn't want to listen to her inner voice. "This is crazy," she would say, "I have no idea where I would go!"

Of course, Maggie didn't know where she would go. Her inner Yes and No are just like my inner Yes and No and your Yes and No. It is clear, without any plans. If we listen to this inner guidance system, we will then take steps to create plans.

"But what if it's all wrong, what if I can't support myself, what if I'm not happy?"

Yes and No can't give us a crystal ball about the future. Those are things we need to work out as we go along. Yes and No are not a life planner, but more like a life definer. Yes and No bring definition and boundaries to our life. Once we have a definition, we can begin to make the plans.

Maggie could ignore her inner Yes and No, the voice telling her to leave the marriage. She could ignore it because she doesn't have any plans made, but this is how we make a plan. If we wait around until the plan is delivered in the mail to us, we will miss many things in our life.

The truth is that Maggie doesn't know what is next. All she knows is that when she listens to her inner voice, she knows she needs to leave her marriage. She doesn't want to watch her husband poison himself with alcohol every night. She can't watch it any longer. She doesn't know what will happen next. She doesn't know if she will ever be happy. She is willing to listen to her Yes and No and not demand plans. She will FIO - figure it out. She knows she is happy riding her bike and she wants to live somewhere warm enough to ride her bike all year round. She begins to look for biking communities.

Not everything is going to work out perfectly. When Maggie decides to make such a big leap in her life, she will face some big financial challenges. Just because she knows how to listen to her Yes and No doesn't mean life won't have challenges. It doesn't mean she won't have problems.

Life is life.

When we listen to our inner Yes and No, we create a customized life, one that really fits who we are. Maggie is looking for a biking community. Her life is going to change dramatically, but she will be living the life that fits her, not the life that fits her husband's alcoholism. That is his life. When she goes in pursuit of her life, she finds it has nothing to do with alcohol or television.

Davis is able to create a life with his partner while listening to his Yes and No. Davis' mate also wants what is best for Davis. He will find a way to workout with him. They both feel that having more quality time together is a priority. They are patient and willing to work through one thing at a time, finding help for grandma, hiring some housekeeping help, and letting a neighbor teen help their daughter with homework one night a week and school projects on weekends.

It takes them a year to get to the point where they are getting quality time together as a couple.

Making the plans to follow through on your Yes and No will take time. There is no magic wand to wave. Expect to do the customizing, the figuring-out.

Jen realizes that she has had lots of experience figuring things out and customizing, but she has made her life fit around the men she has dated. None of her effort to build a life has been around her own soul. She actually has had lots of experience with building a life; it just wasn't actually her own. Rather than thinking about all the things the men are interested in, Jen needs to spend time with herself and be willing to try things that may fit her. She is unsure of what her interests are, she has no confidence she will find the answer.

I remind Jen that as long as she is breathing, she has a soul within to connect to. This relationship with her self has been ignored and of course, Jen fears she can't make this connection. Jen will need to be patient with her ignored self. It may take awhile to show itself to her. She has cast it far away from her view and now she must bring it closer.

Keeping the body physically nurtured and comfortable is essential. Journaling, art, and meditation are all ways of listening to the inside. Jen will be developing her inner-sight. Every now and then she will catch glimpses of her soul appearing, and if Jen is patient with herself, that shut down self will trust that she is finally listening and it will emerge.

For all of us, there is a recovery process to truly recover a relationship with our soul/spirit. The recovery process is about listening, trusting and establishing a genuine relationship with-in. "With-in" brings both parts together: we are with ourselves and it is an inside experience. To keep and hold this connection with-in, we need to set boundaries with everything else. The needs of others, the demands from our lives, can easily consume all of our time and attention.

Apply it:
Draw a picture showing how far or near you feel you are to the soul with-in.

Write down the daring, bold, Yes or No you have inside that you don't yet have a plan for.

Think about the things you have done that have taken patience, time. Put a "P" for patience on your list next to the things that will take some patience to achieve. Are you willing to be patient with yourself?

Journal notes:

Journal notes:

Journal notes:

Chapter 11

After you have done all the hard work of self-care and going with-in to listen to your Yes and No, the next big hurdle is managing the emotions that are unleashed. I am not yet talking about all the emotions that will come at you from other people. That is in a later chapter. I am talking about the emotions with-in.

The emotions can feel like a huge tornado ripping you apart from the inside. Maggie may have gotten clear on her Yes and No but she is also afraid of starting her life in the new customized way. Jen is afraid too. Stu is afraid. I am afraid. You are afraid.

We all fear not being liked, disappointing someone, not being loved. And when I say fear, I mean anxiety, panic, sweating, and trouble breathing.

There is some risk involved in boundary work. There is no way to actually be setting boundaries, to be really doing it, and avoid the emotional storm. The unbearable emotions are part of it. If you are sweating, panicked, nervous, then I can say for sure, you are truly doing it. You are setting boundaries where you need them. People often think if all this emotional distress comes up, they should stop, turn back, and not set the boundary. This is a huge mistake. The emotional distress is not a signal that you are doing something wrong. It is a signal that you are doing something right!

Stuart has to risk stepping outside of his isolation - the safety of his bubble. He learns how to feel his fear, but to keep going forward and connect to other people. He will push through his discomfort to follow his Yes. Yes, he wants to and needs to break through his loneliness. His fear, his discomfort, those are emotions. Those are not his Yes.

Yes and No can be an emotional minefield. Raven feels every single nerve twitching since she has stopped drinking. She is feeling things all the time. It is overwhelming to her. Without the numbing effects of alcohol, Raven feels as if she is standing naked in a crowd at all times. She is easily frustrated and easy to anger. She can't understand why she is angry, but she is angry all the time. Her temper is short and she can't explain why the anger is intense.

What is all the emotional noise about? The emotional noise can feel like a tornado, a whirling spiral that seems to grow bigger the more we think about it. Our emotions will not guide us through the spiral. The emotions just seem to make the whirling worse. Yes and No is the guidance system that will get us through the spiral.

When Wendy is feeling driven to stay long hours each day at work, she has to remember that staying longer doesn't resolve the spiral. It just makes her work longer and harder.

Raven, who is feeling raw in her recovery, needs to know that all that mess of feelings is an emotional mess. It is going to take time for her to sort through the wreckage and find herself. She is going to learn that her feelings are not always sensible or reasonable. They are feelings. The alcohol quieted the mess. Now she doesn't have anything to quiet the feelings. It makes her wonder if maybe she was better off drinking.

I need to reassure her that the mess will be there for awhile. Her emotions need to recover. It is possible that at the heart of it all, she is most angry with herself.

All the years spent covering up her Yes and No have a price when she can finally hear herself.

Stu has also been dealing with emotions for a long time. Through much of his isolating he has been in a dark depression. He has not gotten any help for his depression and let it completely consume him. As he steps out of his isolation, he will need to get help for his depression. It is a thick cloud that can't be ignored.

As we unbury our Yes and No, we need to dig out from under our emotions in order to recover. When we struggle with our boundaries, when we say yes and when we say no, we are often wrestling with our emotions about our Yes and No. We fight and resist putting our boundaries in order because of how we feel about it. Our emotions can be distraught over our boundaries.

Yes and no are not emotions.
Boundaries are not emotions.

Emotions will not guide us through the emotional storm we find ourselves in when we need to set our boundaries in place. The emotions cannot serve as a guidance system for our Yes and No.

Wendy the workaholic has to learn that the thing that drives her to work hard, to overwork, is not an accurate meter. It is not a good guidance system. It drives her into a spiral of exhaustion, no fun, and loneliness because she is working too much. She needs her boundaries to save her from herself. She needs her boundaries to become her guidance system. She will slowly replace her guidance system from the overworking, "can't stop working," to a better system with a stop meter in it; a system that tells her to leave her desk and go play; a system that keeps her phone off on the weekends. To help her set her boundary, she learns to track her work time hourly and to never go past her actual working hours. The discipline Wendy used to work, work, work, will be used to set and follow boundaries instead.

When drinking, Raven's emotions were deadened. Now they are awake and alive. Raven feels a bit out of control. Raven learns to think about where she wants her boundaries. We talk through the expectations she feels from co-workers, friends, and family. We practice anticipating, guessing what others may need or ask of her and figuring out where she needs boundaries. Raven has to meet her boundaries, her Yes and No, for the first time in a long time. She is also introducing her boundaries to the people in her life for the first time.

Getting comfortable with the uncomfortable emotional mess is critical to doing boundary work. Only setting boundaries in your "dead zone", places that are not emotional, is probably completely meaningless. The non-feeling dead zone isn't really where you need the boundary. The hot emotional fear zone – that is where your real boundaries are waiting for you.

I realize this is hard for us because our fear is something we naturally pull back from. It tells us to step away from danger. But when it comes to boundaries, your fear can tell you what to move toward.

Apply it:
Think about some boundaries you have been afraid to move toward.

List those boundaries that you hold inside and avoid because you are afraid.

Pick one from your list to do. Feel the fear and do it anyway.

Journal notes:

Journal notes:

Journal notes:

Chapter 12

Our feelings can be wild and untamed. They are part of our nature. Our feelings need our time and attention. They don't need everyone else's time and attention. They are a correspondence within. Our feelings can be strong and forceful. Understanding and listening to our feelings can create confusion for us when it comes to our boundaries. Things get messy when our feelings are overwhelming us.

Here is an example from Maggie's life that is emotional. Maggie's son is getting married. He does not want dad at his wedding. He has in fact, taken Maggie out to lunch and asked her to come to the wedding alone.

Maggie is overwhelmed by this request. She feels torn about leaving her husband, her son's father, at home and attending their son's wedding without him. She also knows her husband will be devastated to hear he is actually not invited and she imagines he will expect Maggie to stand by his side and not attend. Maggie is so beside herself, all she can do is cry. As we talk through the boundaries involved, we focus on the Yes and No. Her son has decided having dad at the wedding is a No for him. Her son has established his boundary. He didn't pick this boundary to hurt Maggie; he is doing it to take care of himself. He doesn't want to manage his dad's out of control behavior at his wedding.

Maggie is invited to the wedding and she treasures her son and his bride. She is a Yes for attending the wedding. She is sad that her husband is not invited but she understands that his outbursts and rude behavior can be the center attraction.

Maggie's son decides he will tell his dad that he doesn't want him at the wedding and why he has decided this. He is taking full responsibility for his own boundary. The conversation with dad doesn't go well and dad shouts that neither he nor his wife will be attending the wedding. Maggie explains to her husband that she is going to the wedding and wouldn't miss it. Her husband is furious about her decision and refuses to speak to her for days. It is a form of punishment for her deciding Yes, she would go. Her boundary is not where her husband wants it.

These sort of messy things can happen with boundaries. Once our emotions are tangled in it, we can get confused about what our own real and true Yes and No are and struggle to put our boundaries where other people want them, especially when it involves family or work. These are people we want to please or take care of or support.

Our story with Maggie could be different if Maggie did not want to attend the wedding without her husband. It would only be her true boundary if that is what SHE truly wanted, not doing so just because that is where her husband wanted her boundary.

Our emotions can confuse us about our boundaries. Sometimes we want to please someone more than we want to listen to our boundary. We think pleasing someone is where our real and true boundary should be. This is when we drive over ourselves and ignore our inner voice. The voice is there. The boundaries, the Yes and No, are there to take care of you – but only you. Our boundaries are not factoring in other people. Other people have their own boundaries to take care of themselves. Our boundaries are not designed to stretch over and take care of them.

Boundaries are not made of spandex. They are made of Yes and No.

Your boundaries may not get the approval of someone else. If your boundaries are only based on what other people will approve of, you will lose that connection with-in. When we make our boundaries based on approval of someone else, we are connecting to them, not us.

The approval to say Yes and No is NEVER EVER going to come from the "outside", or from other people. The approval you need is from the inside.

You are the only one who can give yourself permission to truly listen to your Yes and No.

Sacrificing Lisa has never really even thought about her own needs. She has arranged herself, her life, and many of her decisions around what will work best for someone else. She has mastered the art of arranging herself around her husband. This is a hard thing to do.

Lisa complains that really listening to her-self is the hardest thing she has ever done, but the truth is that what she has been doing is also hard. She has done it for so long, she thinks it is easy.

She has contorted herself and her life in such a way that even she wonders what happened to her dream of going to school. What happened to her career? As her husband has dumped her, she is forced to hear her own voice.

I always find it miraculous that our inner voice is still there, waiting. It seems that no matter how far we have gone ignoring this voice, it remains alive. Lisa's buried-alive voice is still there.

Raven, who nearly drank herself to death, poisoning her innermost voice with alcohol, can get sober and learn to listen.

Davis has been too busy meeting needs he felt were more important than his own. Davis has learned that he can't measure his needs against someone else's. It is not a contest. Davis has a daughter and a mother who can't take of themselves. That is a fact. His daughter and his mom need him to provide the care he provides. Davis can take care of others, but he must also take care of himself. He must put in some boundaries to protect some time and energy to meet his needs. Davis' life was out of balance because he wasn't caring for himself or doling out miniscule doses of care for himself and saying that should be enough. But his inner voice was saying that wasn't enough. He became depressed as his inner self suffered from the lack of nurturance.

Sometimes we don't want to hear what the inner voice is telling us. When we ask ourselves, "What do I need?" I find very few people like the answer. We harshly dismiss our needs as unreasonable, too expensive, not enough time, ridiculous and selfish.

Davis' emotions took over and sank him into a depression. He felt guilty about taking care of himself. He had depression and guilt arguing with each other and either way Davis would lose. His emotions could not take care of him.

His boundaries could take care of him.

The simple fact is that we take care of our emotions. Our boundaries take care of us.

Taking care of their emotions is completely new for Davis, Lisa, Maggie, Stuart, Jen, Wendy, and Raven. It may also be completely new for you. It helps to have an image of your emotions. An image could be a crying baby, or you may see a piece of art that sums it up, such as the painting, "The Scream" by Edvard Munch. An image could be of a season such as winter, or a landscape. When I am overwhelmed by emotions, I find comfort going for walks in the woods. The presence of the trees reminds me that life is long and these emotions are temporary.

Apply it:

Draw two circles on a page. One circle is inside the other circle. In the innermost circle, put images or words that describe how you feel during an emotional storm inside. In the circle around it, place the things that bring you comfort, mantras you can say to yourself, things you can do that are soothing to your spirit.

When we are in an emotional storm, it is important that we practice saying soothing things to ourselves, mantras, rather than repeating the negative thoughts over and over. Negative thoughts will not help.

When you are in an emotional storm, write down the thoughts you are saying in your head.

Next to it, write some words of comfort, mantras, to repeat over and over.

Journal notes:

Journal notes:

Journal notes:

Chapter 13

Other people, family members, friends, coworkers, neighbors, do not maintain your boundary. Other people show you how strong your boundary needs to be. You will notice that everyone responds or reacts differently to your boundary. If someone notices and recognizes and pays attention to your boundary, it makes things easier. When people are not respecting your boundary, you need to make it clearer. You don't have control over how strong or how high you need to make your boundary fence. Other people show you how high and how strong they need it to be in order for them to recognize your boundary.

Davis told his partner Rob, "No, I do not want a dog." But Rob kept bringing up how good a dog would be for their daughter and a companion for grandma in the house. Davis said he frankly didn't need more chores, to feed and walk the dog. Robert ignored Davis' boundary, his "no", and brought home a Labrador retriever puppy.

When Rob ignored his boundary, Davis caved in and accepted the puppy into the household. What else could he do?

For Davis to hold firm on his boundary and discuss with his partner the issues raised when he is ignored, requires work and focus on their relationship. When Davis "caved," he taught his partner that his boundaries don't mean much to him. It is predictable that Davis is going to feel pushed and ignored often in the relationship. The damage will be to their closeness and intimacy over time. Davis will not feel heard. He will withdraw sexually as well because he won't trust Rob any longer. Sexual intimacy in committed relationships is based on trust. There will also be damage to Davis' relationship to himself. There is a price he pays to his connection within when he ignores his own Yes and No. If Davis does this again and again, he will feel like Raven did, completely cut off from himself. Raven drowned herself out with alcohol, but you actually don't need alcohol to drown out your inner Yes and No.

We can push over our own boundaries and if we do this over and over again, it becomes hard to hear anything at all from inside. It takes determination to keep holding our boundaries and supporting our inner Yes and No even when we don't feel the support from our partner or friend or other people in our life. Most people aren't taught how to respect your Yes and No. They don't just automatically know how to do this. You are responsible to teach people what your Yes and No mean to you.

Some people learn quickly. Other people don't learn quickly at all. You will notice that some people in your life have a hard time with your boundaries. It is not your fault. It is your responsibility to mind your own boundary. Not everyone wants to raise puppies. We all have different boundaries.

Davis explains to Rob that he feels unimportant. He can't handle the idea of a puppy right now. He understands that Rob wants a dog and they discuss that it is important for both of them to be ready for this. Davis is too overwhelmed right now. Rob agrees to find a different home for the puppy. They agree that in a year, they will re-evaluate whether there is or isn't enough help around the house to take on another responsibility. Davis says he can imagine a grown dog, maybe one from the shelter, rather than a puppy. They will revisit this conversation a year from now in April. They also agree to again rearrange their chores at home to try and lighten Davis' load.

Davis feels heard and respected. Rob is taking time to hear how trampled he feels and realizes that there may be other things to focus on rather than a puppy.

This experience of holding to his boundary, while emotionally difficult, does result in better understanding. If Davis did not hold his boundary, there would be less understanding and a pattern of withdrawal would begin, making their entire relationship difficult and perhaps unbearable.

While Davis was overwhelmed and anxious to hold his boundary, this is often what many people go through when they need to hold their boundary or strengthen their boundary. It is like lifting heavy weights. We must work harder, much harder, when someone is not getting our boundary. We must put much more effort into making it clear.

The result of the effort can have a big pay off. Other people may understand you better. Other people may not always like your boundary, but it is yours, not theirs. Other people do not set your boundaries. You do. Only you know what is a Yes and No for you.

Lisa allowed her husband to set her boundaries for her. Then she resented his choices. She wanted him to choose what she wanted. Waiting for someone else to create your boundary where you want it is an impossible way to establish your boundaries. Other people cannot do this for you.

Stuart realizes that he has become isolated and withdrawn from people because he felt they were always pushing on his boundaries.

He thought he was the only one who had to struggle to be heard. He gave up trying. As Stuart learns that setting boundaries is something everyone does all the time, and that the hard part is hard for everyone, he feels encouraged to get more involved in life.

For a long time Stuart, has wanted to be part of the museum and park near his home. He would like to volunteer. We talk about how this is a good opportunity to practice his boundary skills. Stuart is able to anticipate some of the boundary issues that may be part of volunteering, things like time, the kinds of tasks he may asked to do, and the skills he could offer to help this organization. Stuart really doesn't like asking people to make donations and we talk about other skills he could offer to support the museum and park.

He likes hands–on things and wants to be involved in cleanup at the park and cleanup with events at the museum.

This first step for Stuart will also bring him in touch with people and he will have the chance to "join in" to events and establish new relationships. Joining the volunteer crew may not be enough to create the connection he is seeking. He has picked a "place" to make a connection, and it is a start. He needs to have relationships inside the "place". As he thinks about creating relationships, he isn't sure the other museum volunteers are "his people". He is interested in joining a church that has a big social calendar for its members. This second idea is on target for Stuart. By knowing his goal is to break his isolation, he could explore ideas and see if it will help him reach his goal.

The museum, it turns out, is not an ideal place to break his isolation. It is largely a "quiet zone" that does not encourage the interaction he needs. I ask Stuart to research the museum further and find a highly social part that he could get involved in. He chooses the Summer Nights At the Museum planning committee. This committee has the task of making the museum a highly social place. This is a perfect committee for Stuart. He will also learn from them how to set himself up for the social interaction.

The church that is bustling with activities is an endless way for him to make connections. Stuart has learned to not be passive about what is a Yes for him.

Apply it:

It takes determination to stick to our own Yes and No. Where in your life would you like to increase you determination?

List one or two specific things where you will practice holding your boundary.

These can be small things or bigger things. The purpose is to practice sticking to your boundary.

Journal notes:

Journal notes:

Journal notes:

Chapter 14

Other people do not maintain your boundary. Other people will push up against your boundaries and when pushed, you may give up your boundary. You can be talked out of your own boundary. Things go better when you expect other people to struggle with your boundary. You must prepare to hold your boundaries firm. It is not the job of other people to maintain your boundary. They maintain their own boundaries. It should never ever surprise you when other people push your boundaries or fight with you to change your boundary. Expect it.

Lisa's husband had an agreement with Lisa that she would get her turn to go to college as soon as he finished. But when he finished, he wanted to put his income towards a house, not her education. He pushed on her boundary. She caved and moved her line for college.

Other people push on our boundaries all the time. It is not just in big ways. Your boundaries are pushed in small ways all the time. It can happen all day long. It may even be part of your job at work to find yourself dealing with boundary-pushers all day long.

Couples find themselves in small boundary disagreements all the time. These are harder to notice than the big obvious ones. If I say, "I don't want to take calls for the next hour," and my husband brings over the phone and says, it's Lands End about your clothing order, I shake my head, refusing the phone and continuing to knit. Then I become angry with him for "not listening" to me in the first place when I said no calls, please. These "not listening" arguments that couples have are often rooted in boundary disagreements.

Who gets to decide the boundary? Who decides if the boundary should be pushed? My husband thought I'd want the information from the Lands End store about my sweater order. He was evaluating for me, not valuing my boundary. I could call Lands End after I had a little break.

We are constantly trying to figure out "how important is this boundary?"

Other people may not think your boundaries are important. In Lisa's case, she didn't think her own boundaries were important. In hindsight, she says she kept thinking there would be a time when her husband would believe her education was important. She kept waiting for him to take care of her needs. She thought surely one day he would. That day never came. Lisa was shocked. She thought he was selfish. He was selfish but that is not the only reason why he didn't support her going to school. She did not require it. She did not say this was a boundary for her. She did not stand firm.

Trying to teach everyone around you to be more thoughtful is a hard way to get your needs met. It is great when your life is filled with aware, thoughtful people who spend their time thinking about what you need. Expecting this awareness from everyone around you is unrealistic and you will find yourself angry and frustrated with the people closest to you. If you are angry that your employer or life partner or kids don't think about what you need, the good news is: you are the only one who needs to think about what you need.

It works much better to stay aware of your needs and tell people your boundaries. They don't have to guess and miraculously figure out what you need. You just need to be clear and tell them.

The tricky part is other people respecting your boundary. They may not.

When Lisa's husband wanted the house, she just needed to say, "No, I waited to start school and that is what I need to do." Her husband may be angry and throw a fit not getting his way. People often throw fits and get angry with us when we say No.

So what?

People give up their boundaries all the time because other people get angry.

In an earlier chapter, we examined powerful emotional storms. I do not recommend using emotional storms to decide your boundaries. I certainly do not recommend you use other people's emotional storms to determine your boundaries.

When other people get angry about your boundary, it means they can see your boundary. Stand up and take a bow. You have been heard! It does not mean you should change your boundary for them. But often, people do.

It is normal for other people to try to push and manipulate your boundary. Expect other people to push on your boundary. It is helpful to think ahead about how the people in your life might try to manipulate your boundary. If you were going on a trip to somewhere warm and sunny, you would pack your bag for the weather you would expect. You may pack sun lotion, a bathing suit, sandals, a hat, etc. It is useful to "pack" for your boundary as well. Think about what "might" happen. Expect to be pushed.

Perhaps you set a boundary that you were going to leave your office at 5:00pm, but you know there are always one or two emails that come in at 4:55pm from your boss and you try to get these done before leaving. These extra email requests put you at half an hour to an hour of overtime without pay.

This exact scenario was happening to Jen at work. She decided to set her email message to say at 4:45 p.m., "I will return at 8:00 a.m. and respond to emails when I return." She also sat down with her boss and explained that she won't be staying late any longer to fulfill the requests coming near the end of the day. Her boss laughed and said, "I was just sending you my list for the next day. I was not expecting you to stay!"

This conversation was clarifying to Jen. She thought ahead about how to ask her boss for the lists earlier in the day and it turned out her boss was trying to be early, too.

Usually when we sit down with people and discuss our boundaries, we learn interesting things about what other people are expecting or not expecting. Sometimes the expectations we are trying to fill aren't expected at all. This is of course not always the case. Sometimes people have expectations that we simply can't fill.

You can't fulfill everyone's expectations. You can clarify your responsibilities and understand what is required and what is requested at your job.

Sometimes you need to evaluate if it is realistic or if it is too much. Workaholic Wendy never said the demands of her job were too much. As Wendy started setting boundaries on her work and creating limits, she found that her boss and coworkers were angry and disappointed in her. Wendy found their expectations of her would not shift as she made changes. She began looking for a new job. Her goal was to establish performance expectations and hours required at the beginning, at the interview. She found herself checking the reputations of different offices before applying for positions. It took nearly a year and a half to find the right place for Wendy to work. She kept her current job until she found her new one. The culture of the new office was different than what she had experienced. Wendy faced grief as she realized that all along she had a choice. Her employer did not define her boundary, she did.

We don't have a choice about how firm we need to be about our boundaries. The firmness is determined by whether or not others listen. Wendy would have preferred to stay at her old job if only she could have gotten agreement about reducing her load. She changed jobs because she couldn't get agreement. She changed jobs but she kept her boundary. She didn't change her boundary to accommodate her job.

Apply it:
How do you get manipulated?

What new boundaries will you practice holding firm, even when pushed?

I am using the word "new boundaries" though these may not seem new to you. But if you haven't upheld them, then they haven't yet become boundaries, so we will use the word "new". It helps to tell people, "I have not really upheld this boundary in the past, but I'm going to now."

Journal notes:

Journal notes:

Journal notes:

Chapter 15

While all of us will experience having our boundaries pushed, it is important to remember that part of setting a boundary is holding that boundary when pushed. Expect to be pushed.

Other people are not better or stronger than you are. When they push on your boundary, you show them that the boundary is indeed firm. As you saw with Davis and Jen, they went into an emotional spiral when needing to hold their boundaries over work and puppies. They both discovered that their boundaries would be respected if they held on to their boundary. Other people may not even be aware of your spiral and the sweat you are going through setting your boundary. Jen discovered that her boss wasn't expecting all the end of day requests to be filled on the spot. Though Rob was pushing Davis to agree to a puppy and even brought the puppy home, Davis stood firm that he was not taking on the responsibility of a puppy.

In most situations, you will set your boundary, you will experience someone pushing on your boundary, and when you hold firm, the issue will be resolved. Others may or may not like your boundary, but remember, your boundary is in place to take care of you and your boundary can't possibly take care of them. As you hold firm to your boundary, the other person will accept your boundary.

There are some exceptions to this.

You may find that there is one person or several people in your life who, even when you hold your boundary, continue to push, argue, throw a tantrum, act out of control, and refuse to accept "no" for an answer. They call you over and over, wanting to share their thoughts and feelings, or completely ignore you unless you do what they want.

There will be situations when you are setting a boundary with someone who is an expert at manipulation. There are people who have high demands and they feel entitled in some way to have you meet their needs. For whatever reason, they learned to get what they want in the world by being demanding. I have a name for these people. I think of them as extreme challengers. These extreme challengers are not just pushing on you. They push to get what they want from other people too. These are people who may be addicts, alcoholics, or people with mental health distortions.

Addicts, alcoholics, and people with mental health conditions are not good at meeting their own needs or their own responsibilities and they can put lots of effort into getting you to manage their responsibilities. People who think they have authority over you are another group of people who may be manipulating those around them. They are powerful, authoritative, or wealthy and using their power to manipulate people around them.

Extreme challengers have some things in common. They can be demanding and expect you to serve their needs. They tend to trample over your boundaries. These are the people that most of us have the most difficult time with.

When I work with people on setting boundaries, I find it is important to separate out setting boundaries in extreme challengers from setting boundaries with all other people.

Some ways to recognize an extreme challenger:
Is the pushy behavior a pattern?
Have you seen them be pushy often?
Do you hear them expect people to serve them or take care of problems for them?
Do they expect you to handle their responsibilities?
Do they seem to have one problem after another?
Do they seem unable to solve their own problems?
Do they act like you "owe it to them" to solve their problems?

When setting boundaries with extreme challengers, it requires focusing on your goal and practicing skills that are effective with extreme challengers. It is like climbing Mount Everest. This is a difficult mountain to climb and you must prepare for it. The same is true for setting boundaries with extreme challengers. You must prepare for the demanding behavior, the anger and rage and hysteria that ensue when you say, "No."

Some people grew up in families where extreme challengers were their family members. Other people find they are married to an extreme challenger. You can't change the fact that someone is unreasonable, demanding, and manipulative. But you are absolutely required to know this about someone. You need to recognize Mount Everest when you are standing in front of it.

You must prepare for the extreme challengers. The most important way to prepare is to expect manipulation and tantrums when you set a boundary. Do not expect respect or understanding. If that happens, great, but rarely does that happen with addicts, alcoholics, and people with mental health distortions. Part of their distortion is that they believe you are supposed to meet their demands.

Addicts, alcoholics, and people with mental health distortions need to hear your boundary more often than other people. They need repetition. Prepare to repeat yourself.

At one point in my career, I worked in a special school for teens with severe mental health issues. I was assigned to a class of kids that often became violent when told "no". I had a tee shirt made for myself and I put it on, over my clothes, every single day. On the front it said, "Oh well." This was a favorite saying from one of the students. On the back of my tee shirt it said, "No deals."

This group of students were used to making "deals" with teachers about sitting and doing schoolwork. My tee shirt made it clear, the classwork was not a negotiation with each student. It reminded them that I was not negotiating all day on every assignment. The tee shirt helped remind me, as well, to not fall into negotiations all day. This tee shirt is an example of how I needed to prepare for the extreme challenges each day. When there are people in your life who are highly manipulative and demanding, it can be exhausting. At some point, you may not have the energy for Mount Everest.

Maggie believed for a long time that she was causing her husband's unreasonable behavior. She learned that he was an extreme challenger. He would tantrum and argue and demand that everyone just give in to his demands. He expected Maggie to stay home from their son's wedding. It did not occur to him to offer to go to treatment and get help for his problem and promise to be sober by the wedding. It would never enter his mind.

He was demanding that Maggie stay home and when she refused, he began a campaign of not talking to her for days and then weeks.

Extreme challengers try to wear down your boundary. They will hold out until you give in.

In the past, Maggie has gotten caught up in trying to end the fight by giving in. It was always more important to her to have peace in her home. Peace at any price.

Maggie did not give in this time. This will make no impact on her husband. The only one this will help is Maggie. Maggie will practice not giving in under extreme manipulation. Maggie only hurts herself within when she caves in under manipulation.

Raven, Stuart, and Davis spent their childhoods surrounded by family members who were extreme challengers. Davis' father was abusive and out of control. Stuart's father died at a young age from a stroke, leaving his mother alone to raise him. She withdrew into herself, suffering from anorexia, and speaking incoherently, finding herself hospitalized multiple times for her mental illness. Stuart was raised taking care of her when she was not in institutions, and then he was placed in foster care when she was too ill to be home. Raven had two parents who were heavy drinkers. Both parents were into a wild party scene and there were no boundaries in her childhood between adults and children. Raven was overexposed to an adult world of parties, drugs, and drinking.

Extreme challengers will trample the boundaries of anyone within reach. They are not selective: adults, children, parents, employees and employers.

The first key to dealing with extreme challengers is recognizing them. You will need to use the strategies that we discussed earlier, plus a few more that are essential in these situations. I will discuss those strategies in the next chapter.

Apply it:

Who in your life is an extreme boundary challenger?

Journal notes:

Journal notes:

Chapter 16

If you have someone in your life who is an extreme challenger, an expert at manipulating your boundaries, you need to use specific boundary skills. You will be using the first skill that we use for any circumstance: self-awareness (know your own Yes and No); boundary awareness (decide your boundary); and emotional awareness (experience your feelings but don't move your boundary because you are afraid, nervous, sweating). We use those three for all boundaries. In an extreme challenge, we use three additional skills.

The first skill for an extreme condition is to define your responsibilities. In addition to your boundary, you must be clear about the things for which you will take responsibility and things you will not. In extreme challenges, there is often a "dumping" of responsibilities onto you. These responsibilities may include financial responsibilities, as well as others.

Since the dumping occurs regularly, you need to prepare for this and define clearly how much responsibility you will assume. As more and more responsibility gets pushed over to you, you need to push those back and allow the consequences to happen for the challenger.

This can be frightening. There are consequences when someone dumps their responsibilities. They often lose their job, their housing, their partners. You can't possibly hold their world together. When people walk away from responsibilities, there is no way you can carry all of their responsibilities for them. The important thing is to define what you can and can't take responsibility for.

As you clarify what is your responsibility and what is not your responsibility, keep in mind that if you have an alcoholic or addict in your life, responsibilities are confusing for the family. Addicts have problems with responsibility. Addicts often avoid certain responsibilities in their life. Sometimes they avoid all responsibilities, but not always. Often they avoid specific responsibilities, repeatedly. Recovery is always a process of assuming responsibilities. Do not get in the way of someone's recovery by carrying his or her responsibilities.

People are often astounded as they notice how much trouble a recovering addict has with responsibilities. I find it is helpful to guide recovering people and their families to focus on responsibilities and be clear about your boundaries.

In addition to always being clear about your responsibilities, you need to focus on being realistic about what you can and can't take on.

It helps to also think about what responsibilities are reasonable and healthy for the recovering person to carry. I have never met a family that can agree upon reasonable responsibilities for the recovering person. This line is often blurry, and many times I have heard treatment providers also suggest things that keep the recovering person shielded from their responsibilities. I have heard parents told to pay rent for their 35-year-old adult child for a year, while the 35-year-old attends outpatient treatment three times a week for 6 hours total, but does not hold a paying job.

I highly recommend that a therapist support you in setting boundaries when you deal with an extreme challenger. If the challenger is in recovery, I don't recommend using the treatment provider for your own care, as you will need someone to help you with boundaries. Be clear that you are setting boundaries and allow yourself some support as you get help figuring out how to let other people take responsibility for their life, their choices, their decisions, their actions.

How you manage your time is another key boundary skill in an extreme challenge. A time boundary is when you pre-decide how much time you will spend listening or being with a person. You may decide to have lunch every month with someone in your family who is challenging and that lunch will be one hour. When you have a person who abuses the telephone and demands access to you for long periods and repeatedly, it is ok to give them your time boundary. I will return your call on Sunday and I will have 15 minutes to chat.

I am careful with the phone, because I could end up on the phone all the time. I am clear about short conversations. You could become a hostage of someone who consumes your time if you are not watching your time and setting limits. Practice setting time limits and stick to them. It is easy to resent other people if they suck up all your time. Really though, you are responsible for your time.

The final skill for extreme challenges is to define your access boundary. Since I am a therapist, I work with people when they may be going through a rough time. I work with many people and it is not realistic that I can be available all the time. I am clear with people about when I am available, what time of day I return phone calls, and that I am not available, for example, when I am in session with someone else.

In my practice, I sometimes hear from people allowing access to themselves, which they later resent. They need a vacation from work, they are on vacation, and yet they are responding to emails. Who is responsible for defining access to you? You are.

It is important to define access to people in your life. If someone seems to overly access you or contact you more than you want, it is ok to explain to them that it doesn't work for you and give them a boundary around when you are available and when you are not.

Defining responsibilities, time and access can feel harsh to people. Remember that your boundaries are here to take care of you, not someone else. If you are getting drained, overwhelmed, exhausted, or resentful, you are not being clear about your time, your responsibilities, and access to you. It makes people uncomfortable to say no, to set limits on time and responsibilities, but the gains are worth it. People show you how clear you need to be with them.

Raven worked for a Senator who had both power and personal wealth. This Senator, unfortunately, was a person who had no regard for Raven's personal time. In fact, during

139

the years that she worked for the Senator, she can't remember ever having a two-day weekend. He called her or emailed her at all hours with every thought in his head. If he was at a dinner party on the weekend, he would send her a list of things he wanted her to remind him about. He considered her hours' on-demand and all the time.

Raven's drinking increased in this situation as she felt the only way to have a break from her boss was to have a drink. The Senator did not have any boundaries with regard to Raven's time. Raven did not know how to talk about boundaries. She wanted a personal life. She wanted her time off to be off. But she felt it was impossible and in the Senator's realm she felt everyone who worked for him was expected to serve his needs, whenever he had them.

Raven felt her only option was to look for another job. She did not feel like she could get the Senator to respect her boundaries or limits. Raven would not try to set limits with him because she noticed that no one else around the Senator set limits with him.

Raven decided her boundary would be to quit her job. It was a boundary she could control and would protect her from the Senator. She did have options, which would be to stay and insist that he respect her boundaries and limits regarding her time and access. If he felt he could not, then she would need to resign. But she felt that trying to stay and work within limits would be an exhausting struggle for her and could make her sick. She did no want to fight for her boundaries regularly.

Raven felt like she had paid a big price for working for the Senator. Her drinking was out of control and her life was out of her control in every way. Starting with treatment, recovery and looking for a new job felt like the best strategy to her and in her mind it solved the problem.

I wish I could solve every extreme boundary challenge this way. Just eliminate the person from your life. More often, that is not an option. Most people have to find ways to wrestle with the challenger and protect their boundary.

Setting limits on your responsibilities, your time, and your access, is the only way to face a challenger.

There are times when you have choices and there are times in an extreme challenge when you do not. The distinction is when someone is physically ill or mentally limited; that is, unable to make their own decisions. Perhaps they have suffered a stroke or are impaired in a way that qualifies them as disabled. They may be undergoing cancer treatment or something equally as serious and are limited in their ability to manage for themselves. It is essential that responsibilities are shifted to and shared by their family. This shifting of responsibilities needs to be done with some thought about what is realistic. Getting help, allowing people to share the load, is important because the person who takes too much is likely to also become overwhelmed, lose their self-care essentials, and become sick.

Sometimes we must carry more. That is reality. However, I often see situations where the person carrying the most can accept some help, and they are not utilizing the help that is available. When your responsibilities increase, accept help. The most important thing you can do when you are carrying extra is to recognize this, get some assistance, and be sure to do some things that nurture you.

Apply it:
Think of an extreme challenger. Define your responsibilities, your time, and access. Clarify whether your extreme challenger is someone who is truly ill and needs to be cared for, or if this is someone who is capable but insists and

demands that you carry their responsibilities because they refuse to behave responsibly.

Journal notes:

Journal notes:

Journal notes:

Chapter 17

When people are in an extreme boundary challenge, the challenge is about meeting their needs or your own. Their needs are so consuming that you usually can't do both. You can't meet your own needs and meet theirs at the same time. You recognize this consuming nature of the challenger because they basically will take everything you have and suck you dry.

Deciding on a boundary with an extreme challenger can be confusing. I recommend using three guiding questions when you are dealing with extreme boundary challengers:

1. Can I afford it?
2. What will the consequence be for me?
3. Do I have extra or spares of this resource I am giving away?

When Lisa put her husband through school, she worked for eight years paying a college tuition bill for an education that was not her own. It was not something she could afford. She did not have extra money or a spare eight years to give away. She could not have guessed that he would leave her in the end, but she could have realized that at the end of eight years, he would have an education and she would not.

Lisa's story happens all the time to people. We find ourselves giving more than we can afford. We love someone, we care about her, we want to help, but many times we are giving more than we can afford and paying a price for it.

Lisa needed to let her boundaries take care of her during those eight years. Her time and effort could have gone into her own education, and if she had some extra, she could have given him what was truly left over to support him, too.

Imagine if Lisa had set a boundary and let him take loans for his tuition and pay those with his future earnings and at the same time, she took her earnings and went to school. How would she have felt at the end when he left her? I am guessing that she would have been left with at least more of herself at the end. It is also possible that the marriage might have been stronger had she stood her ground and invested more in herself all along. Her own belief that she was valuable enough to invest in may have created a different type of marriage. He, too, might have seen her as valuable and not been dismissive of her.

I can't promise that if you take better care of yourself in your relationship your relationship will be healthier – there are many dynamics in couples. However, the relationship can't turn out well if someone is in a sacrificing position at all times. They will be taken advantage of.

Lisa did not have an easy way to learn this lesson. Some of our boundary lessons are hard to learn and we can pay a high price to learn them. It is a valuable life lesson and hopefully, Lisa will learn that she is not the spare part for dreams of another person. Lisa had to learn about boundaries to see that she had a part in what happened to her. She was not just completely used by her husband. She freely gave more than she could afford to him.

Couples can easily get beyond their boundaries with money and debt. Davis and Rob are living way beyond their means financially. Neither of them is facing the issue and it is a growing problem under the surface of their relationship. They are buying things: clothes, cars, food from an overpriced store. They are spending more than they bring in. They are jeopardizing a secure future. Davis and Rob are afraid to talk about money. They know they both need boundaries and a budget. They may need to say no to themselves and their excessive spending.

Burying the issue is not going to help them. Deep inside, they are burying their Yes and No by going with short term, in the moment, immediate gratification. But in the long term, it is not gratifying. In fact, when the bills come in, it is terrifying to think about the accumulating interest on their credit cards.

As Davis has been digging out his real Yes and No, he realizes that the financial issues he and Rob are not discussing must be faced. He is overwhelmed with how out of control they are regarding money.

When we begin to listen to our Yes and No within, it is completely normal to start a chain reaction. We discover there may be a few more Yeses and Nos deep inside that have been long buried. If you find that your Yes and No lead you on a path to other Yeses and Nos in your life, that is a sure sign that you are listening.

Our lives are about the investments. Our boundaries allow us to make wise investments. Lisa made an investment with her time and money in her husband's education. She believed she was doing it for both of them. But when he graduated Law School, the Law School only gave out one diploma. The Law school didn't ask who paid for the education.

Sometimes it is helpful to check our thinking with the real world. It wasn't "our degree". She wasn't working for the two of them; it was for him. It was a sacrifice on her part. It was a sacrifice that she chose, but the story she told herself was that it was for both of them.

Couples, spouses often use this thinking and it is easy for a partner to lose herself for the sake of the partnership and sacrifice more than she can afford.

While you have a high awareness of those around you, extreme challengers have a low awareness of those around them. Learning how to protect your boundary from an extreme challenger is excellent boundary training. The extreme challengers give us lots of practice. Welcome the practice. Stop wishing an extreme challenger will get it and really understand your boundary. You are not doing something wrong. You are not causing them blindness around your boundaries. Their lack of awareness is not your fault.

A big overlooked consequence that many of us experience is resentment.

It is completely normal to resent the extreme challenger. Resentment is an indication that you are not taking care of you. Resentment is not about them; it is about you. If you have resentment, it is time to face the extreme challenger in a new way. Resentment means you no longer want to go along with what "they want." It means you may not want your thirty-year-old son living in your house. It means you want the unemployed person to get a job, any job, but to begin working and being responsible to pay the bills.

Resentment means you want to say, "No."

Resentment is like a virus that attacks you on the inside. Do not ignore your own resentment. Listen to the resentment; it is leading you to find your real Yes and No.

Sometimes people dismiss their resentment. They tell themselves that it is more important to be a sacrificer or a lover. They tell themselves to ignore their resentment. This is a BIG MISTAKE. Do not ever ignore your own resentment.

The resentment is the healthy part of you trying to get you to pay attention and act differently.

Apply it:
Think of the extreme challenger you are dealing with and ask yourself these 3 questions:
1. Can I afford it?

2. What will the consequence be for me?

3. Do I have extra or spares of this resource I am giving away?

After looking at your answers, what boundary can you set to prevent consequences for you, or relieve yourself of the consequences you are now experiencing?

Journal notes:

Journal notes:

Chapter 18

Trauma and stress will weaken your boundaries.

There are times when you notice that setting boundaries is much more difficult than at other times. Certain people are actually harder to set boundaries with than other people. Our boundaries will be weakened when we are stressed. Setting and holding boundaries is challenging when we feel our best, but when we go through a trauma, a car accident, a death in the family, grief - our boundaries may feel like they have dissolved. We find ourselves saying yes to everything because it is too hard to check in with ourselves. The emotions of grief or distress have filled us up, and we tend to look away from ourselves. As we are engulfed in grief or distress, our boundaries may be hard to hold.

This is normal.

I think the best strategy for this is a prevention strategy. Whenever you are stressed, traumatized, had a loss, accident, death in the family, expect that your boundaries are weak. You need to remember this and pay attention. Know that you are weak and try to limit your exposure to challenges on your boundaries. This is one reason why people who get sober are vulnerable to relapse; it is hard for them to hold their boundary around substances when their boundaries are weakened by stress or trauma.

Stress and trauma are going to happen. All of us will find that our boundaries are vulnerable during stress and trauma and we will find it hard to make yes and no decisions during the trauma. It is helpful to understand what you find "stressful". Sometimes we are stressed and unaware of it. It takes self-awareness to understand what is happening to your stress level inside. You can usually experience signs of stress in your physical body.

My neck becomes rigid when I am stressed. I focus on connecting to my neck several times each day to stay aware of what is happening in the place in my body. This helps me manage stress, release tension, pace myself through the day and take a break when I need to. If something unexpected happens, a stressful event, my stress level will shoot up quickly. But I still need to do the same things: focus on my body, breathe, release tension, pace myself and take breaks when I need to. However, if I had a traumatic event, I will expect that my boundaries are weak and fragile. I expect my neck to stiffen. I expect my boundaries to weaken. I take some boundary precautions. I do some extra protection around my boundaries.

Maggie came home from her bike ride one day, and her husband had to be taken by ambulance to the hospital. His alcoholism had created a blockage in his pancreas and he also suffered a heart attack. Maggie knew he was in late stage alcoholism and that he was at risk of dying from his drinking. She was also unable to "save" him. She visited him each day in the hospital. She was sad and angry all of the time. She thought about her boundaries, her self-care, and knew she did not feel like riding her bike or taking walks. Maggie could have sunk back into her couch or sat by her husband's bedside all day, but she did something completely out of character. After three days and nights at the hospital, Maggie went home for a shower, got some sleep, woke up and went out for a bike ride. She knew that abandoning her self-care was the worst thing for her. She rode her bike for a short ride each morning before going to the hospital. It was just enough to remind her to stay connected to her self-care. If Maggie had not thought about her boundaries, the weakening of them, she would have completely slipped away from herself.

When Raven gets stressed, her boss at work becomes more demanding. She feels she has to work longer hours. On top of that, her car breaks down and she can't afford the repair bill. As Raven's stress climbs, her boundaries get weaker. As her boundaries get weaker, she is vulnerable to drinking again.

Stress weakens our boundaries – this is why stress is a trigger for addicts.

But how many of us have to live with stress? I have never met anyone who doesn't get stressed.

Davis says it actually takes a lot for him to get stressed. Davis thinks he is strong, maybe extra strong. Davis is not actually stronger than you or me; it just takes more for him to become aware of what is happening. Some people do not notice their stress as it builds. They use a blanket of denial to cover over stress. Because it takes "a lot" to notice the stress, Davis probably has lost all sight of his boundaries. He has taken a lot, shouldered a lot, and once again gone way past the point of what he can carry and still take care of himself at all. Davis ends up not feeling stressed, but also not having time for himself, not getting to the gym, no time to read a book. He has lost all of his self-care because he is managing "a lot". He may not be aware of stress, but his self-care has dissolved. It helps Davis not to ask if he feels stressed, but just to notice if he is doing his daily self-care.

It is possible to become numb to our own stress and distress. It turns out that Rob, Davis' partner, is also stressed from his job and sees how overwhelmed and unhappy Davis is, and how much caretaking is needed for their daughter and his mother-in-law. The bills are piling up and Rob doesn't know what to do to dig them out of debt. He just works harder and harder to try to bring more money into the household. His distress is giving him intense stomach pains and he does not want Davis to know that he is having painful stomach cramping that is keeping him in the bathroom for long periods. Rob is avoiding doing much around the house, not because he is oblivious, but because he is in physical pain and does not want to complain. He avoids going home so Davis doesn't see how hard it is for him to move around. Rob is in distress.

Trauma and stress often have a much larger impact on all people who are connected to each other than we understand. Our bodies often hold our distress and we develop symptoms. Trauma and stress blow shrapnel in many directions. If the emotions, the pain is unattended to, it is likely that the person will lose touch with himself, lose touch with his inner Yes and No. The long-term consequences can be extensive. First we care for the emotions, the suffering, the pain, and then we begin to restore or create the connection within to our Yes and

No. This process can take a long time; a period of several years is normal.

Stuart has endured a chaotic childhood and was burdened with continuous trauma trying to manage his mother's severe mental illness. Stuart never really experienced emotional support or nurturance for himself. His isolation from people has been a way to cope with a traumatic life. Stuart does not want to spend his adult years paying the price for the terrible childhood. He realizes there is something else to living; that having relationships with other people won't feel like it did with his mother and he wants to know what is possible. He wants to live beyond the trauma. Stuart is open to allowing himself to feel and experience relationships.

Stuart gets a dog. As he walks the dog, he meets other people with dogs. And people with dogs love to talk about their dogs. This is how Stuart meets Lizzy. Lizzy is an artist and she has a dog. Lizzy and Stuart don't rush into something. It has taken Stuart months to get from thinking about the museum to volunteering, from thinking about a dog to selecting a dog – and I expect that if Lizzy is patient, she will find Stuart worth waiting for.

Apply it:

What events have been traumatic or caused physical distress to your body?

Where do you hold your stress in your body?

How can you take better care of your body and reduce your stress?

What does nurturance mean to you?

Journal notes:

Journal notes:

Journal notes:

Chapter 19

Extreme challenges can't always be prevented or avoided. I was born into a family that had many extreme challenges. In other cases, a traumatic event happens to you; an accident happens, cancer or some other serious health problem strikes without warning.

Davis finds himself caring for his daughter who has some special needs and finds his mother is also dependent on him at this point in her life. Davis has a crucial role to provide the care and support needed for his family. We all have a responsibility to other people in our lives. Depending on how close and connected we feel, we may have a responsibility to several people at the same time.

When Maggie was a new mother thirty years ago, her own mother died a slow and painful death from cancer. Maggie found herself caring for a completely dependent infant while also caring for her completely dependent mother, who was too sick to stand, cook, or clean. Maggie juggled her household and her mother's while her husband came home late and drunk most nights, starting fights and making everything harder. Maggie didn't leave because she didn't have the energy to leave, there was no place to go, and she couldn't begin to plan for her needs while carrying so much in her arms.

The truth is that real caregiving is just part of life and relationships. There are times when you are needed, but you have to ask yourself, is it all the time?

Am I sharing the responsibilities or giving someone a free pass? Am I helping someone who needs to help himself?

These are difficult questions. The first thing we need to do when having extreme challenges is to ask lots of questions about whether or not we are outside of our boundary of responsibility:

1. Is this person truly unable to care for herself?
2. Am I providing housing, food, money to someone who is able to earn his own money?
3. If I am providing care and it is reasonable that I provide it, what am I willing to do to INCREASE my own self-care?

I often meet people who are doing extensive caregiving, but there has been no increase in caring for themselves. In fact, most often I notice people are doing LESS of their self-care while they care for someone else. This is how we lose ourselves – we lose our connection to our own Yes and No. We overburden ourselves with extreme challenges and we don't acknowledge that we also need to provide quality care to ourselves.

As Davis talked with Rob and increased his care for himself with some reading time and some time at the gym, his own mood improved. Davis had slipped into a depression. His own spirit was deprived while he did so much for others and his own spirit was suffered from neglect and abandonment.

As Davis reconnected and showed some care, nurturance, and support to himself, his depression lifted. As Rob became honest about his stomach pain, he realized that he was also suffering from depression and he knew he needed help.

We are vulnerable to depression when we are not caring for ourselves. Lisa believes she was doing self-care all the while she worked two jobs and paid the tuition on her husband's law school. "I went to the gym, I ate healthy foods, I took long runs on weekends while he studied. Why doesn't that count as self-care? Why did I get depressed?"

Lisa's story is an excellent example of how you can be doing everything that looks like self-care but it isn't self-care at all.

Yes, Lisa was doing good things for her body, but Lisa was not taking care of herself financially. She had put herself in a slavish-position. She was working for no pay. She wasn't investing her money earned into anything that belonged to her. She was earning it all for someone else. She wasn't watching out for herself at all. As you think about this, you will realize self-care is a large territory. It can be many different things.

I meet plenty of people who eat well, exercise, and get good sleep and yet they are depressed. I help them by looking beyond the physical issues of fitness and food and I look at how they are meeting their other needs: emotional needs; social needs; how they play; financial needs; where they are pushing or demanding more than their spirit can take.

Please note that many different things can cause depression, but it is always important to get to the root of the depression and treat the root, not just the symptoms. When your inner self watches you take care of others and to a large extent knows that you think other people are more important than you, that inner spirit does not thrive. It withers. Your "inside self" needs some attention and nurturance, too.

Jen thought her partner should refill her when she was on empty. Human beings don't work that way. You can't neglect yourself and then get filled up by other people. Chances are much higher that if you neglect yourself, other people will neglect you, too. Other people can't make up for what you are refusing to give yourself. You can take care of those who need you, but you must take care of you too.

Raven feels overwhelmed by every single responsibility since she has been sober. When did life get so hard? She can't remember things feeling so difficult. Each day she struggles against the weight of her responsibilities and all she wants to do is drink. When Raven drinks, her responsibilities disappear for awhile. She gets a complete break. She can't get that when sober. Raven has to learn how to manage responsibilities without being overwhelmed. Newly sober, she can't really carry all the responsibilities without being overwhelmed.

Raven learns to recognize the overwhelmed feelings and learns how to stop, drop, and roll. She learns to literally stop, drop whatever she is doing and roll - play for a few minutes. Do a Sudoku puzzle; take a walk outside; open a good book. She learns to give herself a break when she needs. She has some thoughts that she carries with her on a little note card. The thoughts are like mantras that she repeats to herself:

I don't need to be afraid.

I have done much harder things.

I will break it down into baby steps. Baby steps, baby steps, baby steps.

Trying to live in small baby steps changes the overwhelmed state of mind for Raven. She sees one thing at a time when she says, "Baby steps." One thing at a time is not overwhelming and the wave inside begins to go down.

If you are not sure how to cope with all the feelings that rise up inside, talking with a therapist can be helpful. When you begin to really dig your self out and establish a real connection to your self, it doesn't always feel good. I promise you, lots of feelings can rise up from a self that has been ignored by you for a long, long, time. That self can be pissed. It can be sad and grieving. If all this stuff comes up for you, it means you are starting to listen.

When we live without listening inside and then we start listening, it may take an extraordinary amount of self-care to deal with your self. It is not unusual in my private practice that I need to send people to physical therapy to help their bodies recover. They may need medical assistance, and lots of time to walk, be within, and get truthful with themselves. It will take an investment in you. It will take time.

Apply it:
Get a pen and paper and answer this question honestly. Let your innermost soul write the answer for you.

I am willing to invest in myself in new ways by:

Journal notes:

Journal notes:

Chapter 20

Throughout this book, you have been following seven people: Raven, Lisa, Wendy, Jen, Davis, Maggie, and Stu. They each have used one particular mode of covering up their real Yes and No. They have each been committed to allow their boundaries to take care of them.

You also have a mode, a way that you have struggled with boundaries: workaholism, caretaking, sacrificing, loving, numbing, isolating, or protecting. You may find that you use a combination of these: sacrificing, caretaking, and numbing; or isolating and protecting; or workaholism, isolating, and protecting. Some of these modes fit together and you find yourself with a couple of strong ways to bury your real Yes and No.

It is also possible that you have recovered from certain modes, ways you used to be in the past, but you no longer struggle with that mode.

I have recovered from caregiving to the extreme. I am still working on my workaholism. I have to stay vigilant on this one and committed to working without overworking. I have learned that what feels like "underworking" to me, is much closer to the best way for me to work. I seem to be symptom free when I work without overworking. If I get stress, or an extreme challenge, my tendency is to work harder. I have learned to ignore that response and instead recognize the challenge and meet it instead with increased self-care. I will schedule more support for myself, more time with friends, more time to walk outside, or knit, something I enjoy immensely.

Practicing boundary work means you ask yourself these questions:
What is my mode?
What are my symptoms – what happens to me when I do my mode(s)?
What is my self-care plan?
How will I increase my self-care and stop myself from doing this mode?

You may find that you need to adjust your self-care plan if it isn't working. People who have used numbing as a mode may have a difficult time using self-care that isn't numbing. It is important to do sensory-based self-care. Be sure your self-care uses touch, taste, sight, movement, smell – anything that involves the senses is going to be important to counteract numbing.

Be accountable to yourself and recognize that you are recovering from your mode to really listen to your Yes and No.

When we live in our mode, we bury our real Yes and No. We cover it and can't get to our true needs. Sometimes we don't like what we find there. We judge our Yes and No. We don't want to listen. We block ourselves from our real Yes and No.

It is essential to end this struggle with your inner compass. Your boundaries are doing one, and only one, thing – trying to take care of you. It is OK to let your boundaries take care of you. It may not meet your expectations of yourself. You can't care for as many people as you want to, without caring for yourself.

Every time we ask ourselves to care for others, we must also increase our care for ourselves. The problem is that most people will do less for themselves as they care for others. Some people think it is impossible to care for others and themselves at once. It may be that you are doing more for others than is possible. It may be that you are doing not as much as you think you are in the long run.

Maggie wasn't truly taking care of her husband. If she truly had been able to do that, he would be sober.

We really need to question our caregiving sacrificer at times to be sure we are helping someone who needs our help, not just robbing others of the life lessons they need to learn.

When you have extreme challenges, it can be harder to maintain an inner connection to your true self, your real Yes and No. The challenges outside of you can consume you. The only way to get through extreme challenges is to strengthen your own connection to you first.

Belay is a term used in rock climbing. I think of this term when facing extreme challenges. In rock climbing, you belay; you tie yourself securely to something while you climb steep and treacherous rocks. During extreme boundary challenges, belay yourself to you. Stay securely fastened to yourself at all times. Expect there to be conflict with yourself as the challenge becomes more challenging. It is harder to stay true to your real Yes and No, and you may feel like abandoning yourself to care for someone else instead.

Do not abandon yourself.

If you ignore your true Yes and No, if you try to bend your Yes and No into the non-truth, twist them and squeeze them because it seems too hard to listen to your true Yes and No, you will be at huge risk of having your Yes and No rebel inside. When you ignore your Yes and No, you will get symptoms. You will have trouble sleeping, depression, runaway thoughts, high-risk behavior, relapse, perfectionism – whatever happens to you when you don't listen to yourself, will start happening. You will find yourself using one of the seven modes to avoid yourself. You will find yourself drowning.

Stuart understands that his relationship to his mentally ill mother keeps him extremely challenged. When she does not take her medication, she has episodes. She wanders the streets of L.A. Stuart realizes that he can't supervise his mother. He applies for aid from the state and also hires, with his own funds, some extra support for her to be sure she has her medication and is taken for a walk or does an activity each day. This costs him extra financially but it also gives him peace of mind. He spends Sundays with his mom, but allows himself time to be with Lizzy and do things that he enjoys.

Maggie has had a similar problem with her husband. Maggie spent years losing her life, her relationship to her son, for the addiction her husband lives with. Her husband refuses to get treatment. He refuses to attend AA meetings. He refuses to get sober. Maggie, like Stuart, had a hard time recognizing that her job was to save herself, too. She was busy doing her mode of protecting and she buried her real Yes and No. When Maggie really listened to her truth, she realized she was angry. She was outraged at how many years she had spent in a fog with her husband. To dig herself out, Maggie had to do three things: she had to forgive herself for staying in her mode (she simply did not know what else to do); she had to commit to save herself; she had to listen to her Yes and No.

When she listened to her Yes and No, she knew that No, she didn't want the marriage any more, and Yes, she found peace and connection while riding her bike. Maggie knew the protector part of her did not want to leave her husband, but when she stopped living that mode, she couldn't find any other part of her that needed to stay with her husband. She knew his alcoholism was taking both their lives and she realized this was not good for her, nor was it required of her.

Davis unexpectedly developed brain cancer. While Davis had made significant progress with his self-care, the brain cancer required much more of him. Davis thought about his options. He actually worried that for him to be in the hospital and undergo treatment and recovery would be too hard on his family. Rob broke down upon hearing this. He realized Davis was slipping back to his old mindset. When faced with yet another extreme challenge, Davis' first response was his mode: the caregiver. Rob reminded Davis that he needed to make choices based on what was best for his health and well-being, and not anyone else. Robert said he would take over the jobs Davis had with his mom and their daughter. He said, "All those jobs are over." Robert hired some help and prepared to provide everything that Davis would need. He negotiated at his law firm that he would limit his hours, to fully support Davis.

Friends offered to do an overnight shift each week at their house, to provide some care for their daughter and mother, and Robert welcomed the help. Friends provided meals and rides to get treatment for Davis. Their life completely altered. With the tremendous support around him, Davis took part fully in his treatment. He learned about the role of stress on cancer. He recognized that overdoing it for others and his selfless way of living had contributed to his cancer. He realized that his body had limits to what it could endure. Davis learned in his cancer treatment how important self-care would be in his aftercare as well. He had to learn to take exceptional care of himself.

The good news is that Davis had something deep inside of him that was fully equipped to help him: his boundaries, his Yes and No.

Rob also learned about the impact of stress on himself and his stomach pain. He believed the cancer actually saved both of their lives and forced them to make changes that were needed.

Raven works for her sobriety every day. She decided not to look for another job, but instead to go into business on her own. She is doing some communications work, social media, and graphic design. Raven realized she had dreams inside of her that she was going to follow. She laughs that she is just as demanding as the Senator was on her time. But she has preferred learning to set limits with herself rather than the Senator.

There is no way to ever finish our work on boundaries. Paying attention to our Yes and No is an ongoing awareness. We are all going to face challenges at different times. We are going to have difficult challenges to our boundaries throughout our lives. We can't control the challenges or the challengers. We can't make those stop. The only thing we can control is how we respond to the challenges. We can increase our own self-care when we are challenged.

Journal notes:

Journal notes:

Afterword

This book is not ending at the end. You can revisit this book as you need. It is a companion for you on the road as you work with your boundaries, as you start new relationships and when you are looking for your boundaries.

The irony of boundaries is they are not rigid or set like a wall. You are not building a wall. Your boundaries are fluid, dynamic, moving, adapting, as your life changes, as new situations arise, as new relationships form.

Boundaries are often in process, being formed and reformed. As you have challenges and challengers in your life, you may change where you need your boundaries.

Setting limits is sweat.
It doesn't get easier.

You will make better choices, you will think more about what you need.

It may take many reads before you feel like you "get it." I have created workshops and materials to help you with this work. It is a big process.

181

A therapist can be a great support as you build boundaries.

Listen to the stories of other people in your life. You will see that we are all working on our boundaries, all the time. Many people find themselves trying to figure it out without any tools or just repeating the same pattern over and over because they really don't know how to dig themselves out. I have written this book to serve as a guide, filled with tools, to help you dig out your Yes and No whenever you need.

People often ask me about how these tools apply to someone recovering from traumatic stress or domestic violence. When we are exposed to violence and trauma, our boundaries are weaker. If this happens repeatedly, our boundaries may feel shattered. The path to connecting within is the same. We need to be able to connect to our broken shattered selves and listen. Listening to the pain inside may be difficult.

Please be gentle and expect this to be a slow process of establishing trust and connection inside. Restoring or building this connection within will require creating some useful ways to envision building a bridge to the self that is sturdy, reliable, and safe. Working with people who understand what safety is and learning how to protect and care for the self will be the beginning.

I have more to share on all things boundary-related and the more you practice building your boundaries, the more you will want to share.

I look forward to hearing about your journey with these skills.

To the many incredible people who have shared their experiences with me, thank you for bravely listening within. I hope the map I have shared with you helps many others.

Sarri

SarriGilman.com

Journal notes:

Journal notes:

CPSIA information can be obtained
at www.ICGtesting.com
Printed in the USA
LVHW022333280822
727054LV00002B/205

9 780989 778725